Spring-clean those Maths skills with CGP!

Blow away the winter cobwebs with this CGP Daily Practice Book — it'll help pupils' Maths skills sparkle in the spring sunshine!

There's a page of brilliant Maths practice for every school day of the Spring Term, all covering vital skills from the Year 5 curriculum.

It's perfect for use in class or at home, with plenty of examples and splashes of colour to keep things interesting. Bring on spring!

What CGP is all about

Our sole aim here at CGP is to produce the highest quality books — carefully written, immaculately presented and dangerously close to being funny.

Then we work our socks off to get them out to you — at the cheapest possible prices.

Contents

☑ Use the tick boxes to help keep a record of which tests have been attempted.

Week 1
- ☑ Day 1 1
- ☑ Day 2 2
- ☑ Day 3 3
- ☑ Day 4 4
- ☑ Day 5 5

Week 2
- ☑ Day 1 6
- ☑ Day 2 7
- ☑ Day 3 8
- ☑ Day 4 9
- ☑ Day 5 10

Week 3
- ☑ Day 1 11
- ☑ Day 2 12
- ☑ Day 3 13
- ☑ Day 4 14
- ☑ Day 5 15

Week 4
- ☑ Day 1 16
- ☑ Day 2 17
- ☑ Day 3 18
- ☑ Day 4 19
- ☑ Day 5 20

Week 5
- ☑ Day 1 21
- ☑ Day 2 22
- ☑ Day 3 23
- ☑ Day 4 24
- ☑ Day 5 25

Week 6
- ☑ Day 1 26
- ☑ Day 2 27
- ☑ Day 3 28
- ☑ Day 4 29
- ☑ Day 5 30

Week 7
- ☑ Day 1 31
- ☑ Day 2 32
- ☑ Day 3 33
- ☑ Day 4 34
- ☑ Day 5 35

Week 8
- ☑ Day 1 36
- ☑ Day 2 37
- ☑ Day 3 38
- ☑ Day 4 39
- ☑ Day 5 40

Week 9
- ☑ Day 1 41
- ☑ Day 2 42
- ☑ Day 3 43
- ☑ Day 4 44
- ☑ Day 5 45

Week 10
- ☑ Day 1 46
- ☑ Day 2 47
- ☑ Day 3 48
- ☑ Day 4 49
- ☑ Day 5 50

Week 11
- ☑ Day 1 51
- ☑ Day 2 52
- ☑ Day 3 53
- ☑ Day 4 54
- ☑ Day 5 55

Week 12
- ☑ Day 1 56
- ☑ Day 2 57
- ☑ Day 3 58
- ☑ Day 4 59
- ☑ Day 5 60

Answers 61

Published by CGP

ISBN: 978 1 78908 656 0

Editors: Paul Jordin, Duncan Lindsay, Claire Plowman, James Summersgill

With thanks to Tom Carney and Alison Griffin for the proofreading.

With thanks to Lottie Edwards for the copyright research.

Clipart from Corel®

Printed by Elanders Ltd, Newcastle upon Tyne.
Based on the classic CGP style created by Richard Parsons.

Text, design, layout and original illustrations© Coordination Group Publications Ltd. (CGP) 2020
All rights reserved.

Photocopying this book is not permitted, even if you have a CLA licence.
Extra copies are available from CGP with next day delivery • 0800 1712 712 • www.cgpbooks.co.uk

How to Use this Book

- This book contains 60 daily practice tests.

- We've split them into 12 sections — that's roughly one for each week of the Year 5 Spring term.

- Each week is made up of 5 tests, so there's one for every school day of the term (Monday – Friday).

- Each test should take about 10 minutes to complete.

- The tests contain a mix of topics from Year 5 Maths. New Year 5 topics are gradually introduced as you go through the book.

- The tests increase in difficulty as you progress through the term.

- Each test looks something like this:

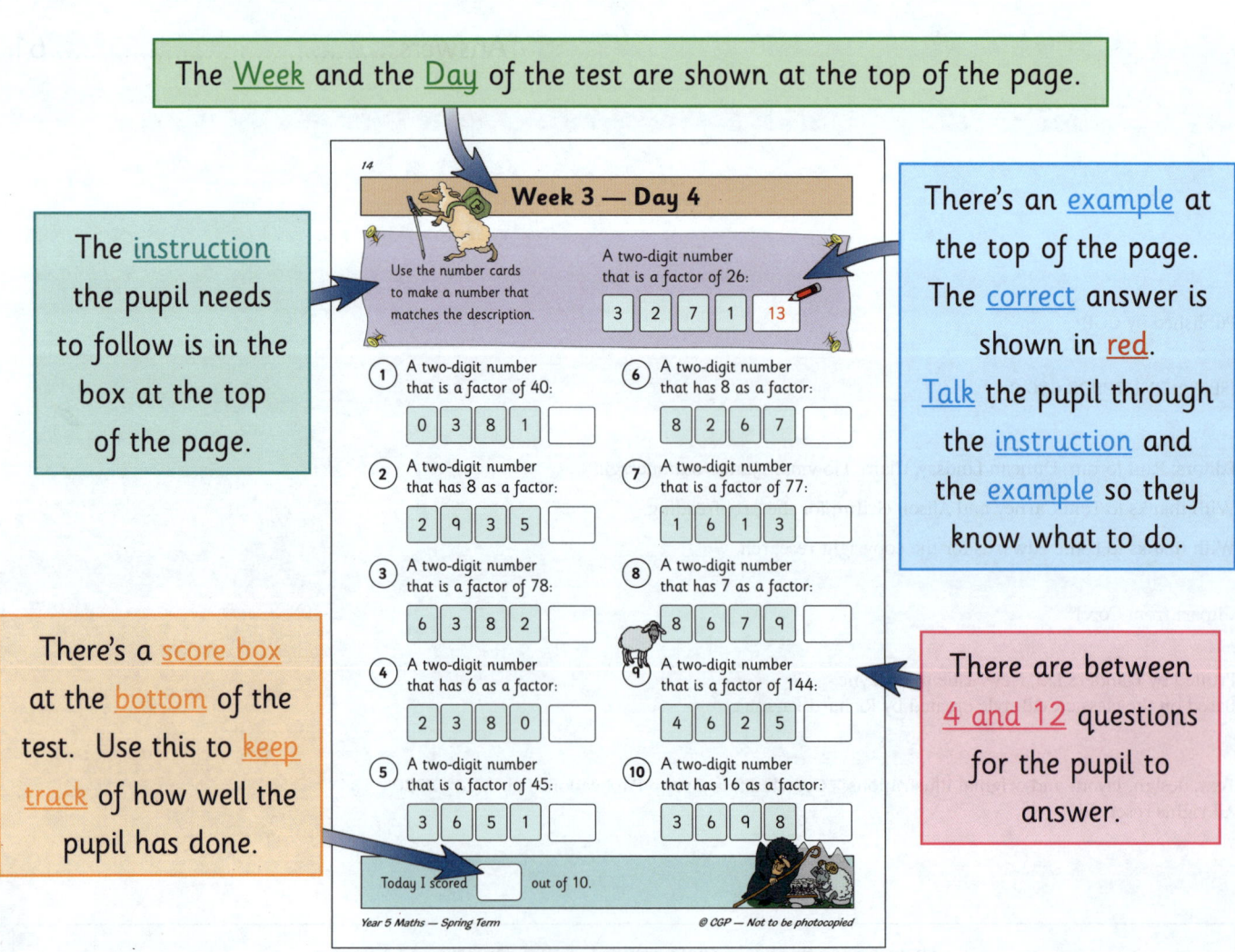

The Week and the Day of the test are shown at the top of the page.

The instruction the pupil needs to follow is in the box at the top of the page.

There's an example at the top of the page. The correct answer is shown in red. Talk the pupil through the instruction and the example so they know what to do.

There's a score box at the bottom of the test. Use this to keep track of how well the pupil has done.

There are between 4 and 12 questions for the pupil to answer.

Week 1 — Day 1

Circle the fraction that is equivalent to the decimal in the box.

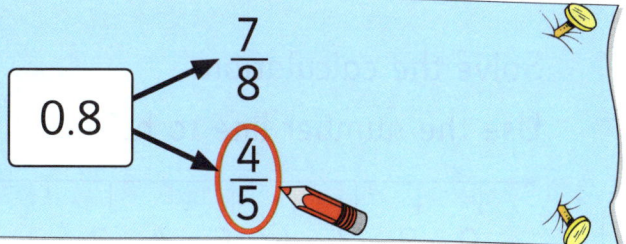

1)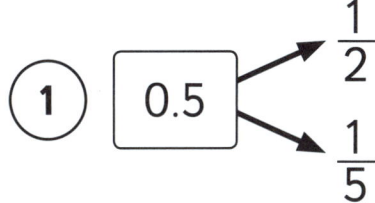

2) 0.25 → 2/5, 1/4

3)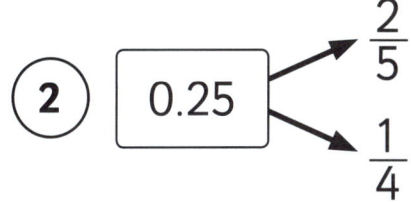

4) 0.75 → 70/100, 3/4

5) 0.3 → 3/10, 1/3

6) 0.2 → 1/20, 1/5

7)

8) 0.25 → 2/8, 5/10

9)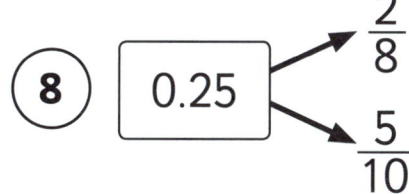

10) 0.9 → 90/100, 5/6

Today I scored ☐ out of 10.

Week 1 — Day 2

Solve the calculation.
Use the number line to help you.

−4 + 8 = 4

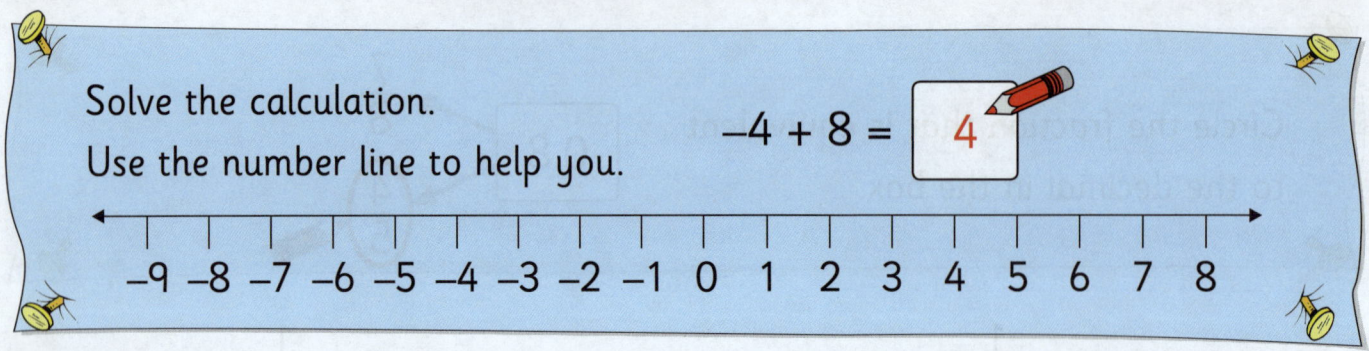

1) −1 + 2 = ☐

2) −5 + 2 = ☐

3) −3 + 8 = ☐

4) −6 + 4 = ☐

5) −5 − 2 = ☐

6) −4 − 4 = ☐

7) −7 + 7 = ☐

8) −5 + 9 = ☐

9) −2 − 7 = ☐

10) −8 + 10 = ☐

Today I scored ☐ out of 10.

Week 1 — Day 3

The bar graph shows the number of pictures Hamish and Rowan drew over 4 days. Over the 4 days, how many more pictures did Hamish draw than Rowan?

5

1.

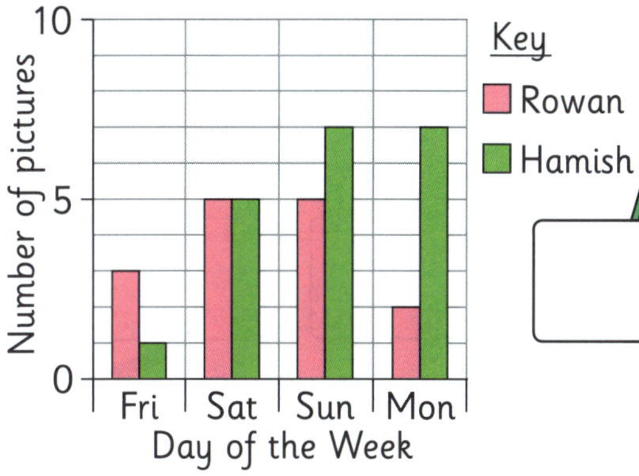

2.

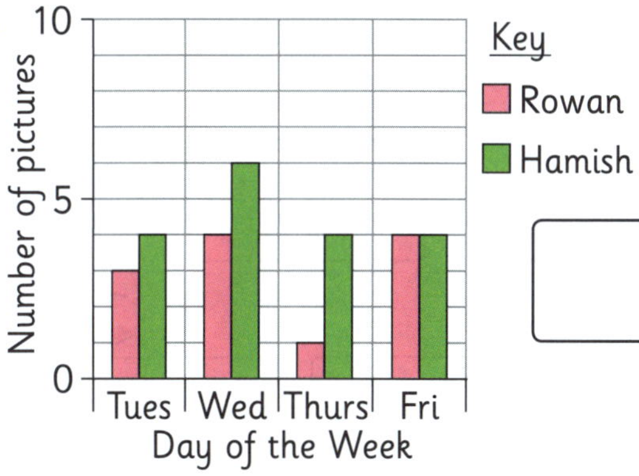

3.

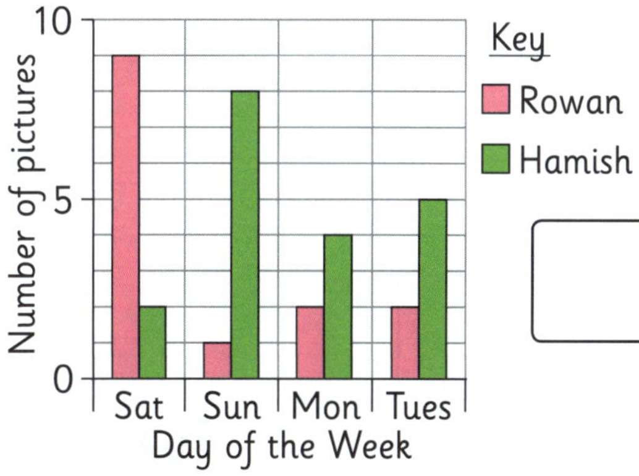

4.

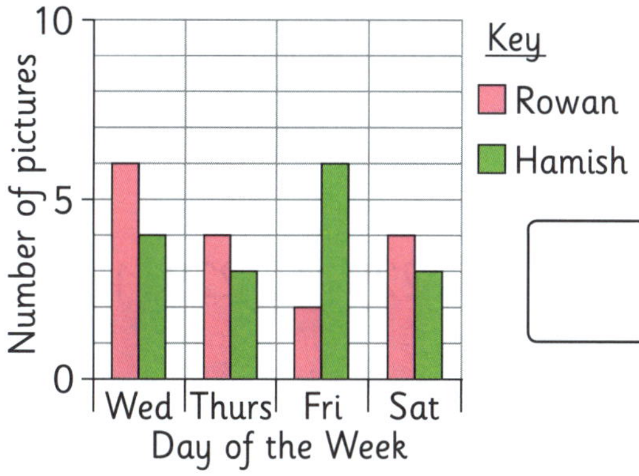

5.

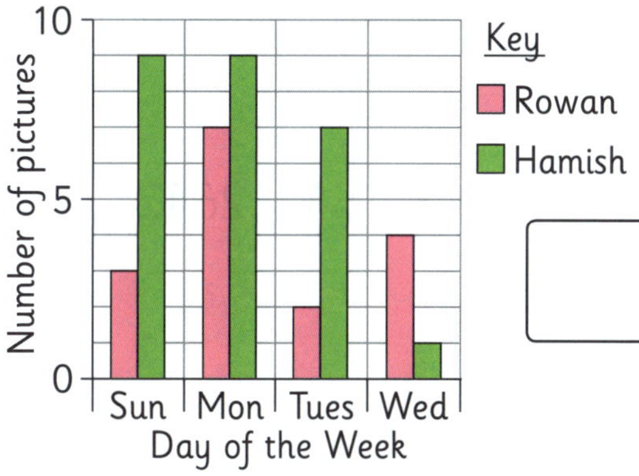

6.

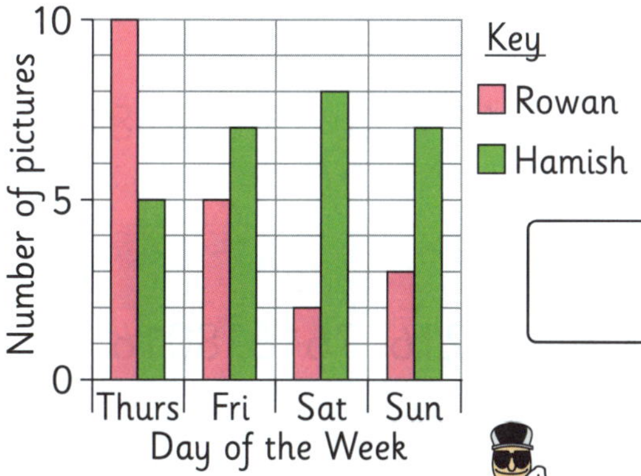

Today I scored ☐ out of 6.

Week 1 — Day 4

Complete the sequence.   3194, 3294, 3394, **3494** , **3594** , **3694**

1) 40 403, 50 403, 60 403, ____ , ____ , ____

2) 3929, 3949, 3969, ____ , ____ , ____

3) 17 229, 16 229, 15 229, ____ , ____ , ____

4) 7536, 7836, 8136, ____ , ____ , ____

5) 442, 1542, 2642, ____ , ____ , ____

6) 88 922, 87 921, 86 920, ____ , ____ , ____

7) 66 823, 75 823, 84 823, ____ , ____ , ____

8) 7216, 7616, 8016, ____ , ____ , ____

Today I scored ____ out of 8.

Year 5 Maths — Spring Term

Week 1 — Day 5

Two students are reading. Tick the box next to the student who is reading faster.

Ali reads 5 pages every 2 minutes. ☐
Biff reads 2 pages every 30 seconds. ☑

1. Cam reads 2 pages every 2 minutes. ☐
   Dill reads 4 pages every 6 minutes. ☐

2. Eve reads 3 pages every 2 minutes. ☐
   Fia reads 2 pages every 1 minute. ☐

3. Greg reads 6 pages every 5 minutes. ☐
   Hugh reads 14 pages every 10 minutes. ☐

4. Ike reads 7 pages every 2 minutes. ☐
   Jill reads 19 pages every 6 minutes. ☐

5. Kat reads 8 pages every 3 minutes. ☐
   Liz reads 15 pages every 9 minutes. ☐

6. Mo reads 8 pages every 4 minutes. ☐
   Noah reads 1 page every 2 minutes. ☐

7. Ola reads 10 pages every 12 minutes. ☐
   Pia reads 3 pages every 4 minutes. ☐

8. Quin reads 5 pages every 2 minutes. ☐
   Rei reads 12 pages every 6 minutes. ☐

9. Sid reads 15 pages every 5 minutes. ☐
   Tori reads 1 page every 30 seconds. ☐

10. Una reads 3 pages every 90 seconds. ☐
    Vera reads 2 pages every 2 minutes. ☐

Today I scored ☐ out of 10.

Week 2 — Day 1

Fill in the missing number. 21 567 is [20 000] to the nearest 10 000.

1) 34 629 is [ ] to the nearest 10 000.

2) 48 805 is [ ] to the nearest 10 000.

3) 55 537 is [ ] to the nearest 10 000.

4) 670 210 is [ ] to the nearest 100 000.

5) 834 019 is [ ] to the nearest 100 000.

6) 256 370 is [ ] to the nearest 100 000.

7) 349 876 is [ ] to the nearest 100 000.

8) 392 471 is [ ] to the nearest 10 000.

9) 435 209 is [ ] to the nearest 10 000.

10) 251 293 is [ ] to the nearest 10 000.

11) 982 001 is [ ] to the nearest 100 000.

12) 897 532 is [ ] to the nearest 10 000.

Today I scored [ ] out of 12.

Week 2 — Day 2

Circle all the fractions that show how much of the circle is shaded.

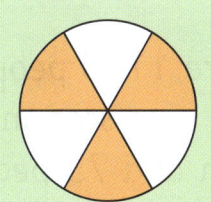 (1/2) 1/3 (3/6) (6/12) 6/14

1

4/9   1/3   2/6   3/15   4/12

5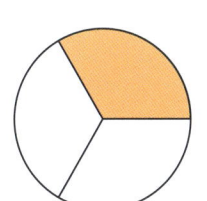

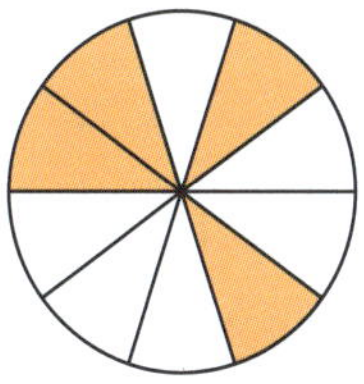

32/60   30/50   2/5   12/20   4/10

2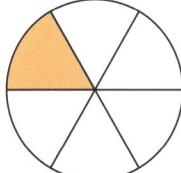

6/12   4/24   3/18   7/30   1/6

6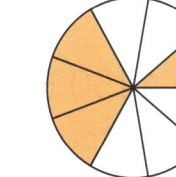

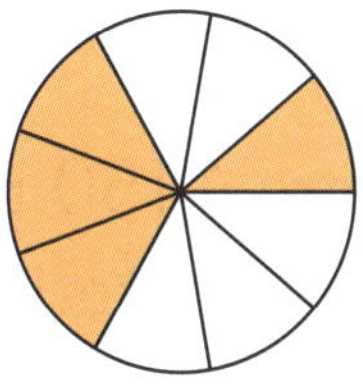

4/9   9/45   6/18   20/90   12/27

3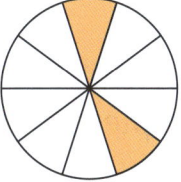

5/30   6/20   1/5   9/40   2/10

7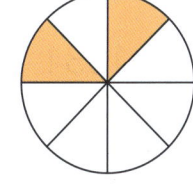

2/8   3/4   9/16   6/24   7/20

4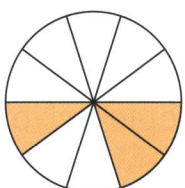

8/20   60/100   18/50   3/10   9/30

8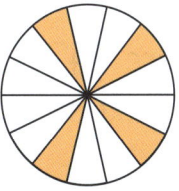

7/28   4/14   12/42   30/70   2/7

Today I scored ☐ out of 8.

Week 2 — Day 3

How many people are on the train when it leaves the station?

There are 1150 people on a train. At the next station 250 people get on and 75 people get off.

1325

1) There are 1398 people on a train.
   At the next station 430 people get on and 620 people get off.

2) There are 1015 people on a train.
   At the next station 357 people get on and 29 people get off.

3) There are 1150 people on a train.
   At the next station 187 people get on and 325 people get off.

4) There are 1235 people on a train.
   At the next station 457 people get on and 29 people get off.

5) There are 1331 people on a train.
   At the next station 93 people get on and 472 people get off.

6) There are 1002 people on a train.
   At the next station 135 people get on and 88 people get off.

7) There are 1477 people on a train.
   At the next station 118 people get on and 92 people get off.

8) There are 1199 people on a train.
   At the next station 189 people get on and 463 people get off.

Today I scored ___ out of 8.

Year 5 Maths — Spring Term © CGP — Not to be photocopied

Week 2 — Day 4

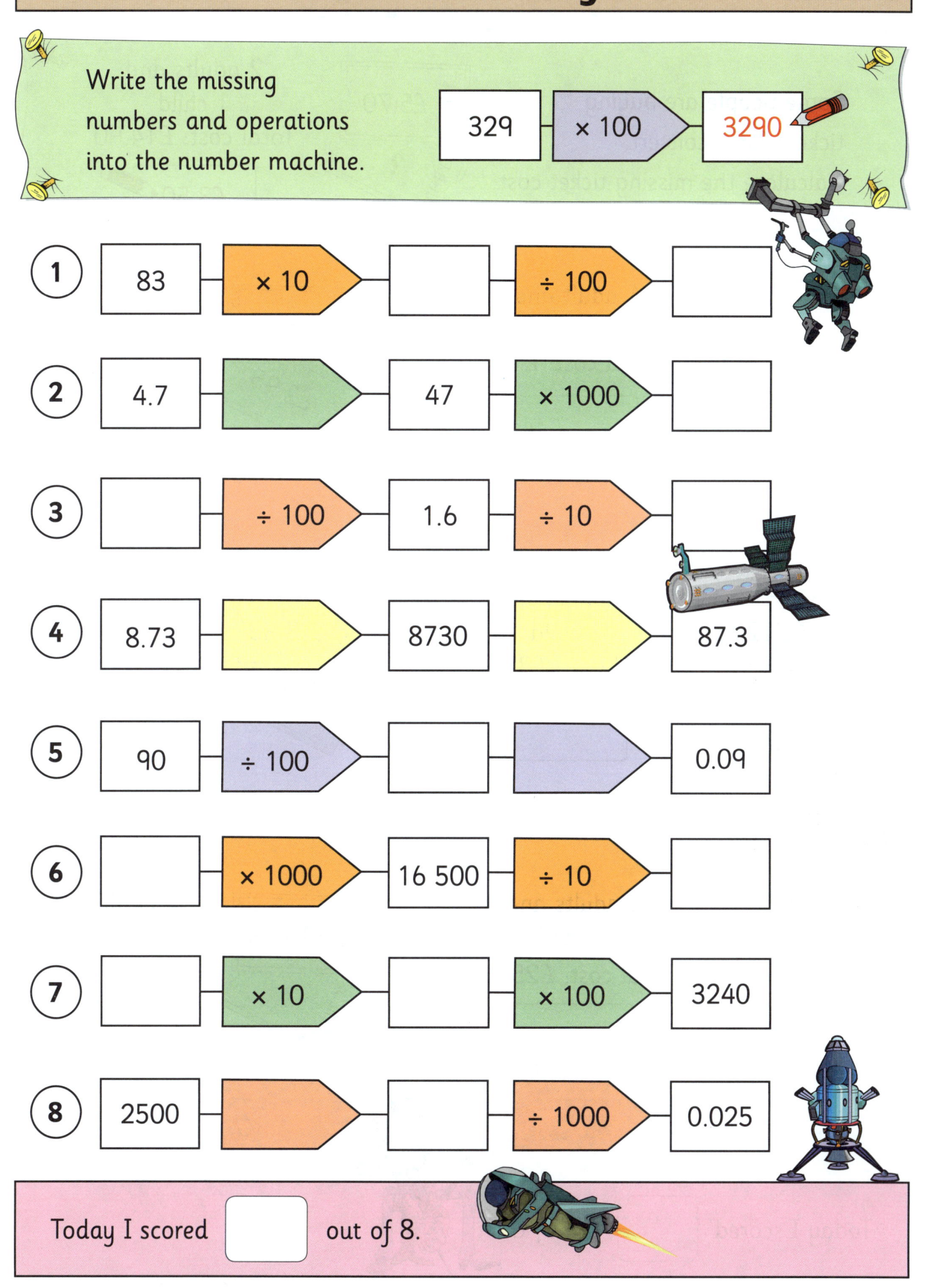

Write the missing numbers and operations into the number machine.

329 → × 100 → **3290**

1) 83 → × 10 → ☐ → ÷ 100 → ☐

2) 4.7 → ☐ → 47 → × 1000 → ☐

3) ☐ → ÷ 100 → 1.6 → ÷ 10 → ☐

4) 8.73 → ☐ → 8730 → ☐ → 87.3

5) 90 → ÷ 100 → ☐ → ☐ → 0.09

6) ☐ → × 1000 → 16 500 → ÷ 10 → ☐

7) ☐ → × 10 → ☐ → × 100 → 3240

8) 2500 → ☐ → ☐ → ÷ 1000 → 0.025

Today I scored ☐ out of 8.

Week 2 — Day 5

Some people are buying tickets for a concert. Calculate the missing ticket cost.

2 adults and 1 child
Total cost: £14.90

£3.50

1  1 adult and 2 children
Total cost: £12

4  1 adult and 2 children
Total cost: £11.05

2   2 adults and 1 child
Total cost: £32.95

5  3 adults and 1 child
Total cost: £48.43

3  3 adults and 1 child
Total cost: £25.30

6  1 adult and 2 children
Total cost: £44.89

Today I scored [ ] out of 6.

Week 3 — Day 1

Write the Roman numeral in figures.   VIII [8]

1) L ☐
2) IV ☐
3) XV ☐
4) XXIII ☐
5) LVI ☐
6) XC ☐
7) LXXVII ☐
8) LXXXVIII ☐
9) XCI ☐
10) XCIX ☐
11) XLIX ☐
12) LXXIX ☐

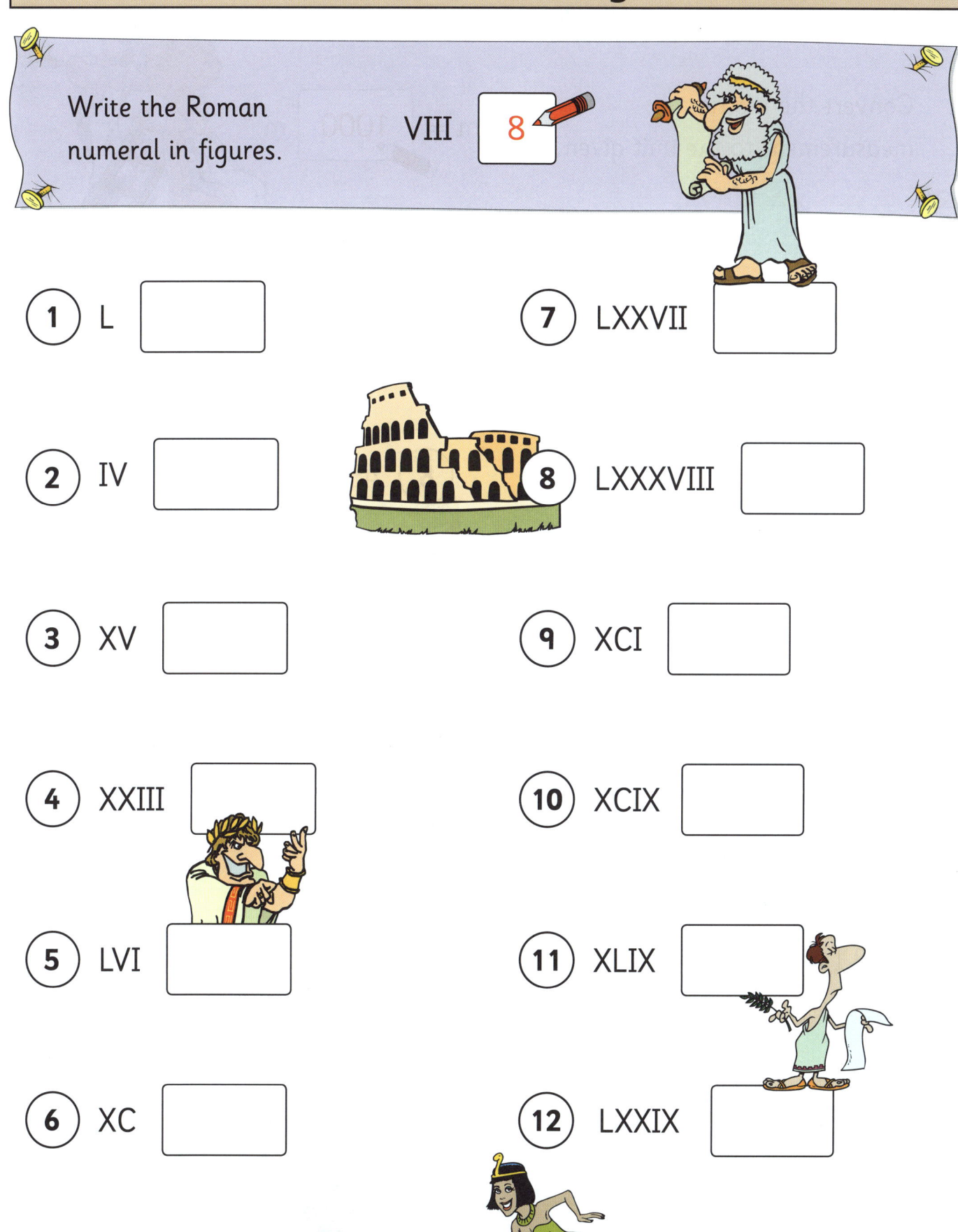

Today I scored ☐ out of 12.

Week 3 — Day 2

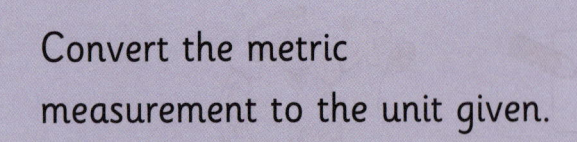

Convert the metric measurement to the unit given.   1 km = 1000 m

1) 1 m = ☐ cm

2) 1000 ml = ☐ l

3) 100 g = ☐ kg

4) 500 cm = ☐ m

5) 3 l = ☐ ml

6) 20 g = ☐ kg

7) 50 mm = ☐ cm

8) 456 ml = ☐ l

9) 8.4 kg = ☐ g

10) 5.51 l = ☐ ml

11) 2998 g = ☐ kg

12) 600 mm = ☐ m

Today I scored ☐ out of 12.

Week 3 — Day 3

Solve the calculation.

28 298 − 4536 = 23 762

```
  2⁷¹28298
−    4536
   23762
```

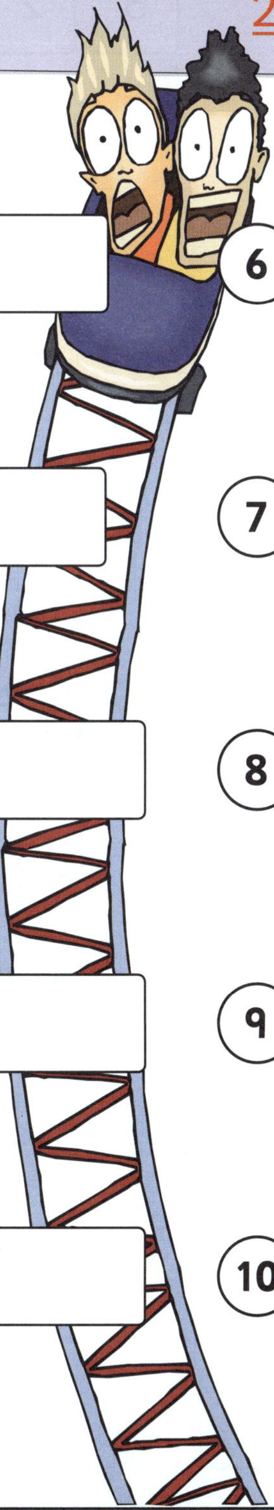

1) 6329 + 2157 =

2) 7038 − 2855 =

3) 99 999 − 2222 =

4) 45 619 + 7248 =

5) 12 121 − 1212 =

6) 64 987 + 7212 =

7) 87 427 − 8538 =

8) 63 734 + 9486 =

9) 12 345 − 9999 =

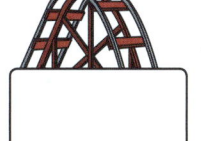

10) 83 257 + 9964 =

Today I scored ☐ out of 10.

Week 3 — Day 4

Use the number cards to make a number that matches the description.

A two-digit number that is a factor of 26:

| 3 | 2 | 7 | 1 | **13** |

1. A two-digit number that is a factor of 40:

| 0 | 3 | 8 | 1 | |

2. A two-digit number that has 8 as a factor:

| 2 | 9 | 3 | 5 | |

3. A two-digit number that is a factor of 78:

| 6 | 3 | 8 | 2 | |

4. A two-digit number that has 6 as a factor:

| 2 | 3 | 8 | 0 | |

5. A two-digit number that is a factor of 45:

| 3 | 6 | 5 | 1 | |

6. A two-digit number that has 8 as a factor:

| 8 | 2 | 6 | 7 | |

7. A two-digit number that is a factor of 77:

| 1 | 6 | 1 | 3 | |

8. A two-digit number that has 7 as a factor:

| 8 | 6 | 7 | 9 | |

9. A two-digit number that is a factor of 144:

| 4 | 6 | 2 | 5 | |

10. A two-digit number that has 16 as a factor:

| 3 | 6 | 9 | 8 | |

Today I scored ☐ out of 10.

Week 3 — Day 5

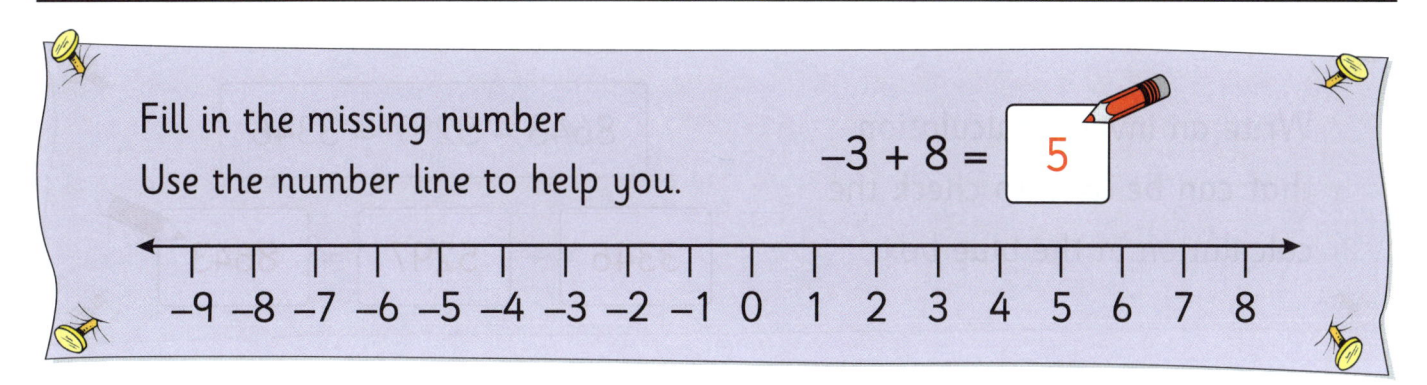

Fill in the missing number. Use the number line to help you.

−3 + 8 = 5

← −9 −8 −7 −6 −5 −4 −3 −2 −1 0 1 2 3 4 5 6 7 8 →

1) −7 + 6 = ☐

2) 7 − 8 = ☐

3) −5 + 13 = ☐

4) −3 + ☐ = 2

5) −9 + 16 = ☐

6) −1 − ☐ = −8

7) ☐ + 7 = 3

8) 5 − 11 = ☐

9) ☐ + 10 = 8

10) 8 − 17 = ☐

11) 2 − ☐ = −9

12) −9 + 15 = ☐

Today I scored ☐ out of 12.

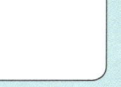

Week 4 — Day 1

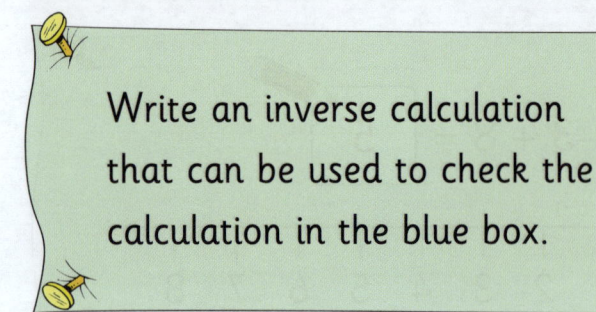

Write an inverse calculation that can be used to check the calculation in the blue box.

8643 − 5297 = 3346

3346 + 5297 = 8643

1) 5842 + 3150 = 8992   ☐ − ☐ = ☐

2) 7712 − 3452 = 4260   ☐ + ☐ = ☐

3) 2998 + 6451 = 9449   ☐ − ☐ = ☐

4) 9027 − 4584 = 4443   ☐ + ☐ = ☐

5) 501 × 10 = 5010   ☐ ÷ ☐ = ☐

6) 636 ÷ 6 = 106   ☐ × ☐ = ☐

7) 242 × 4 = 968   ☐ ÷ ☐ = ☐

8) 992 ÷ 8 = 124   ☐ × ☐ = ☐

Today I scored ☐ out of 8.

Week 4 — Day 2

The table shows some approximate conversions between metric and imperial units. Use the table to complete the sentence.

Metric	1 m	1 kg	1 litre
Imperial	3 feet	2 pounds	2 pints

15 litres is approximately equal to 30 pints.

1) 3 m is approximately equal to ☐ feet.

2) 5 litres is approximately equal to ☐ pints.

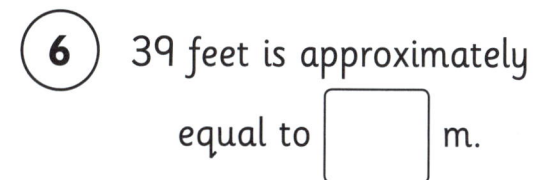

3) 8 kg is approximately equal to ☐ pounds.

4) 9 m is approximately equal to ☐ feet.

5) 13 kg is approximately equal to ☐ pounds.

6) 39 feet is approximately equal to ☐ m.

7) 28 pints is approximately equal to ☐ litres.

8) 42 pounds is approximately equal to ☐ kg.

9) 47 kg is approximately equal to ☐ pounds.

10) 81 feet is approximately equal to ☐ m.

Today I scored ☐ out of 10.

Week 4 — Day 4

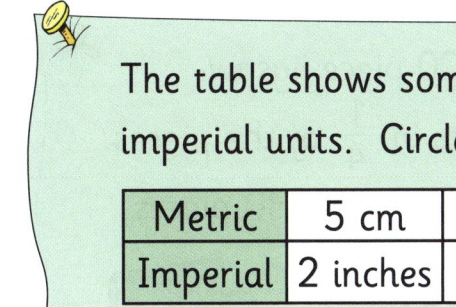

The table shows some approximate conversions between metric and imperial units. Circle the larger of the two measurements shown.

Metric	5 cm	1 l	100 g
Imperial	2 inches	2 pints	4 ounces

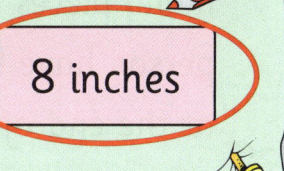

16 cm   (8 inches)

1) 10 cm   3 inches

2) 500 g   5 ounces

3) 4 l   5 pints

4) 12 pints   5.5 l

5) 20 cm   10 inches

6) 10 g   1 ounce

7) 44 pints   25 l

8) 35 cm   15 inches

9) 700 g   30 ounces

10) 55 cm   21 inches

Today I scored [ ] out of 10.

Week 4 — Day 5

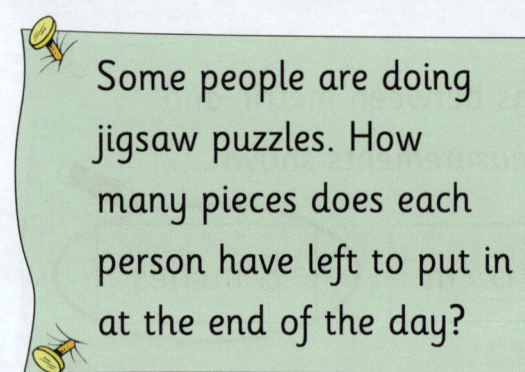

Some people are doing jigsaw puzzles. How many pieces does each person have left to put in at the end of the day?

Ana does a 10 000 piece jigsaw. In the morning, she puts in $\frac{1}{4}$ of the pieces. In the afternoon, she puts in 4330 pieces.

3170

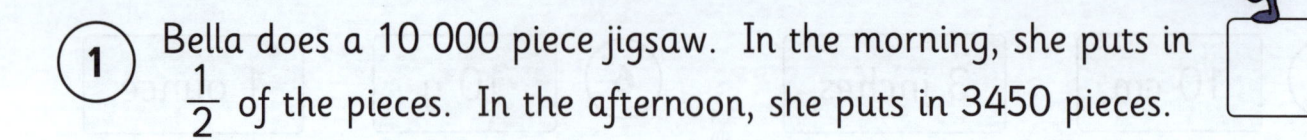

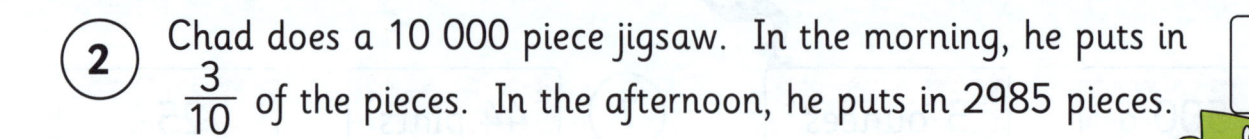

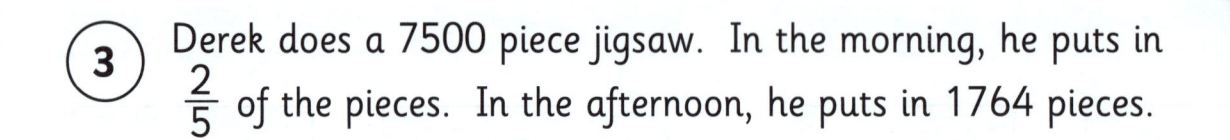

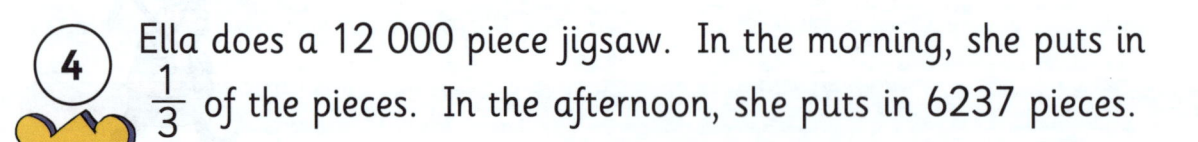

1) Bella does a 10 000 piece jigsaw. In the morning, she puts in $\frac{1}{2}$ of the pieces. In the afternoon, she puts in 3450 pieces.

2) Chad does a 10 000 piece jigsaw. In the morning, he puts in $\frac{3}{10}$ of the pieces. In the afternoon, he puts in 2985 pieces.

3) Derek does a 7500 piece jigsaw. In the morning, he puts in $\frac{2}{5}$ of the pieces. In the afternoon, he puts in 1764 pieces.

4) Ella does a 12 000 piece jigsaw. In the morning, she puts in $\frac{1}{3}$ of the pieces. In the afternoon, she puts in 6237 pieces.

5) Farid does a 8000 piece jigsaw. In the morning, he puts in $\frac{3}{4}$ of the pieces. In the afternoon, he puts in 1649 pieces.

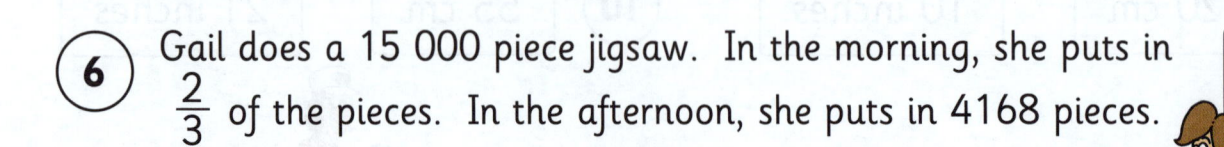

6) Gail does a 15 000 piece jigsaw. In the morning, she puts in $\frac{2}{3}$ of the pieces. In the afternoon, she puts in 4168 pieces.

Today I scored ☐ out of 6.

Week 5 — Day 1

Solve the calculation.   430 ÷ 10 = 43

1) 37 × 100 =

2) 2500 ÷ 100 =

3) 8000 ÷ 1000 =

4) 1.2 × 10 =

5) 78 ÷ 10 =

6) 65.4 × 100 =

7) 1500 ÷ 1000 =

8) 100 × 0.4 =

9) 483 ÷ 100 =

10) 1000 × 3.983 =

11) 4497 ÷ 100 =

12) 79.38 × 1000 =

Today I scored [ ] out of 12.

Week 5 — Day 2

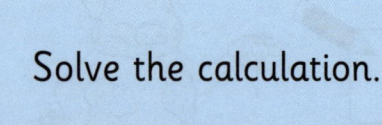

Solve the calculation. $\frac{1}{5} + \frac{1}{5} = \boxed{\frac{2}{5}}$

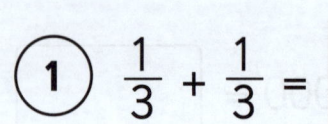

1) $\frac{1}{3} + \frac{1}{3} = \boxed{}$

2) $\frac{2}{6} + \frac{3}{6} = \boxed{}$

3) $\frac{2}{7} + \frac{8}{7} = \boxed{}$

4) $\frac{2}{7} + \frac{6}{7} = \boxed{}$

5) $\frac{8}{12} + \frac{11}{12} = \boxed{}$

6) $\frac{11}{3} - \frac{1}{3} = \boxed{}$

7) $\frac{9}{4} - \frac{6}{4} = \boxed{}$

8) $\frac{4}{7} + \frac{19}{7} = \boxed{}$

9) $\frac{8}{9} - \frac{7}{9} = \boxed{}$

10) $\frac{6}{8} + \frac{7}{8} = \boxed{}$

11) $\frac{9}{6} + \frac{14}{6} = \boxed{}$

12) $\frac{38}{5} - \frac{9}{5} = \boxed{}$

Today I scored ☐ out of 12.

Week 5 — Day 3

Write the number in words.   7450   seven thousand four hundred and fifty

1) 3829

2) 15 107

3) 76 591

4) 44 066

5) 112 000

6) 808 987

7) 100 100

8) 999 999

9) 123 456

10) 440 033

Today I scored [ ] out of 10.

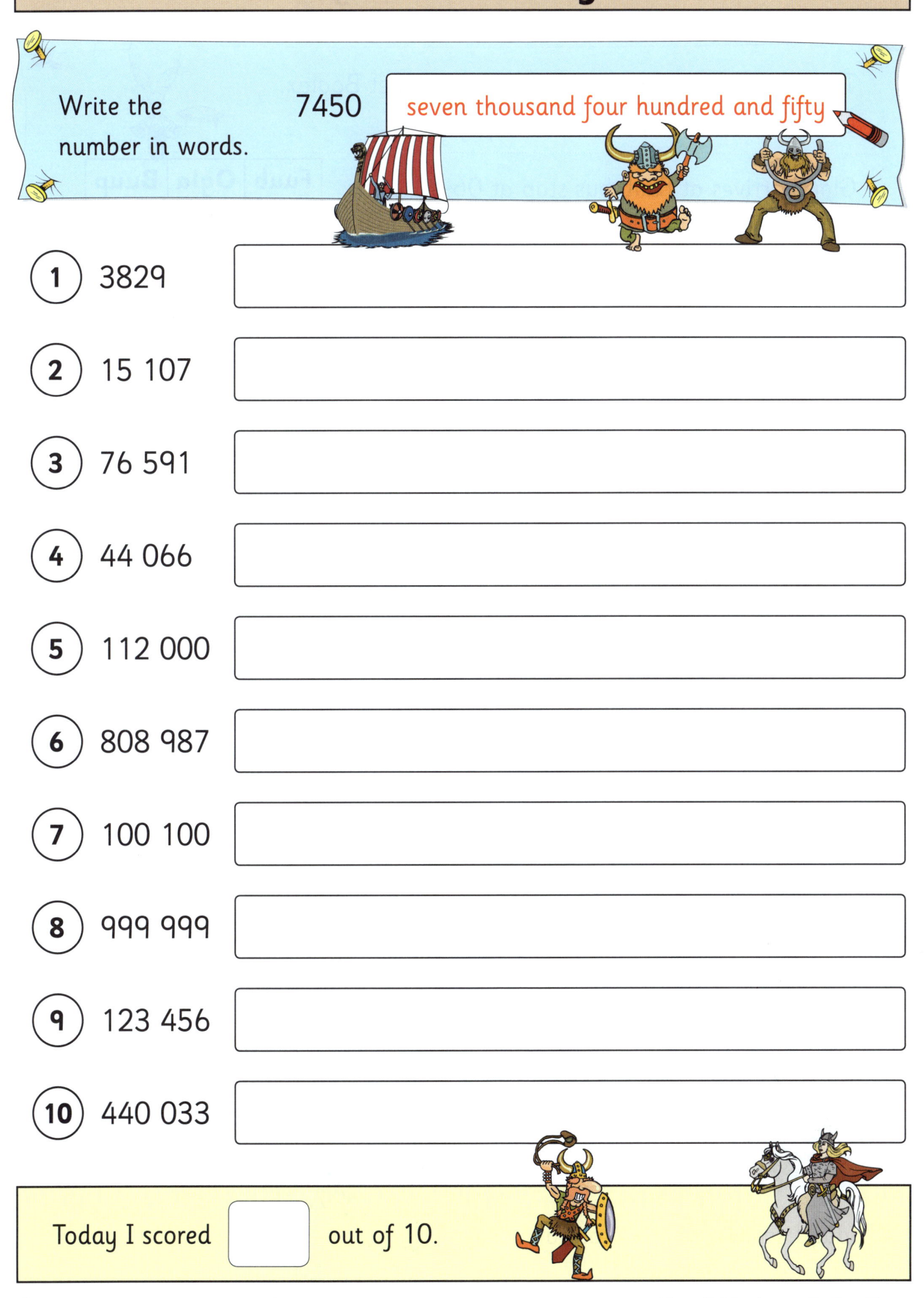

Week 5 — Day 4

This is a space-bus timetable from the planet Boglax.
Use the timetable to answer the question.

Glorgl arrives at Fuub bus stop at 06:40.
What's the earliest time she can get to Ogla?

07:01

Fuub	Ogla	Buup
04:34	04:51	05:11
05:29	05:46	06:06
06:44	07:01	07:21

1) Gork arrives at Fuub bus stop at 07:06.
What's the earliest time he can get to Ogla?

Fuub	Ogla	Buup
07:04	07:21	07:41
07:18	07:35	07:55
07:32	07:49	08:09

2) Greep arrives at Ogla bus stop at 08:15.
What's the earliest time he can get to Buup?

Fuub	Ogla	Buup
08:04	08:21	08:41
08:18	08:35	08:55
08:32	08:49	09:09

3) Nomf arrives at Fuub bus stop at 08:51.
What's the earliest time she can get to Buup?

Fuub	Ogla	Buup
08:47	09:04	09:24
08:59	09:16	09:36
09:15	09:32	09:52

4) Sneggo arrives at Ogla bus stop at 11:21.
What's the earliest time she can get to Buup?

Fuub	Ogla	Buup
10:29	10:46	11:06
11:19	11:36	11:56
11:38	11:55	12:15

5) Parlki arrives at Fuub bus stop at 12:32.
What's the earliest time she can get to Buup?

Fuub	Ogla	Buup
12:07	12:24	12:44
12:31	12:48	13:08
12:39	12:56	12:16

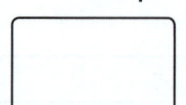

Today I scored [ ] out of 5.

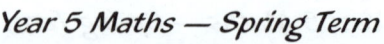

Week 5 — Day 5

The pupils in Mrs Khan's class are working out how long it is until they leave. Fill in the gap using a whole number or a mixed number.

Stevie leaves in $1\frac{1}{2}$ hours. This is the same as 90 minutes.

(1) Jez leaves in $4\frac{1}{2}$ hours. This is the same as ☐ minutes.

(2) Kylie leaves in $\frac{1}{2}$ an hour. This is the same as ☐ minutes.

(3) Ken leaves in 150 minutes. This is the same as ☐ hours.

(4) Lily leaves in $2\frac{1}{4}$ hours. This is the same as ☐ minutes.

(5) Zain leaves in 375 minutes. This is the same as ☐ hours.

(6) Ali leaves in $1\frac{3}{4}$ hours. This is the same as ☐ minutes.

(7) Ryan leaves in 465 minutes. This is the same as ☐ hours.

(8) Carly leaves in $3\frac{1}{3}$ hours. This is the same as ☐ minutes.

Today I scored ☐ out of 8.

Week 6 — Day 1

Fill in the missing time to complete the conversion from 12-hour to 24-hour clock format.

3:45 pm → 15:45

1) 7:20 pm → ☐

2) 2:30 am → ☐

3) ☐ → 17:35

4) ☐ → 20:01

5) 11:59 pm → ☐

6) 11 am → ☐

7) 6:30 pm → ☐

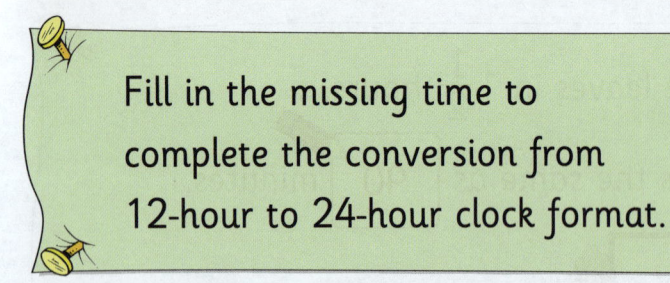

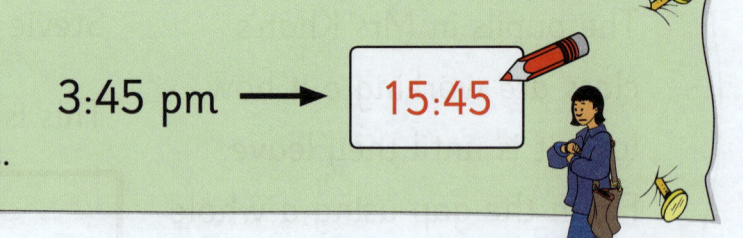

8) ☐ → 22:47

9) ☐ → 19:27

10) ☐ → 13:13

11) 12:05 am → ☐

12) 12:39 pm → ☐

Today I scored ☐ out of 12.

Week 6 — Day 2

Complete the sequence.

Count back in steps of $\frac{2}{100}$.

$\frac{73}{100}$ $\frac{71}{100}$ $\frac{69}{100}$ $\frac{67}{100}$ $\frac{65}{100}$

1) Count on in steps of $\frac{1}{100}$.

$\frac{34}{100}$ $\frac{35}{100}$ $\frac{36}{100}$

2) Count on in steps of 0.02.

0.23   0.25   0.27

3) Count on in steps of $\frac{5}{100}$.

$\frac{25}{100}$ $\frac{30}{100}$ $\frac{35}{100}$

4) Count back in steps of 0.02.

0.8   0.78   0.76

5) Count on in steps of 0.25.

0.25   0.5   0.75

6) Count back in steps of $\frac{4}{100}$.

$\frac{44}{100}$ $\frac{40}{100}$ $\frac{36}{100}$

Today I scored ☐ out of 6.

Week 6 — Day 3

Calculate the missing distance for the triathlon.

Bike 18 km
Swim 700 m
Run ? km
Total 22 km

3.3 km

1) Bike 16 km
   Swim 400 m
   Run 5 km
   Total ? km
   ☐ km

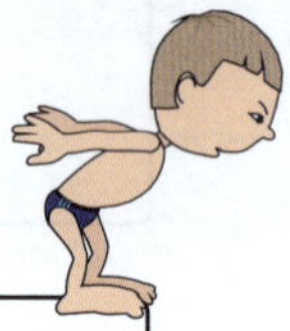

2) Bike 14.5 km
   Swim 500 m
   Run 6 km
   Total ? km
   ☐ km

3) Bike 20.5 km
   Swim 700 m
   Run 3 km
   Total ? km
   ☐ km

4) Bike ? km
   Swim 300 m
   Run 2.7 km
   Total 15 km
   ☐ km

5) Bike 14.5 km
   Swim ? km
   Run 6 km
   Total 21 km
   ☐ km

6) Bike 25.2 km
   Swim 800 m
   Run ? km
   Total 30 km
   ☐ km

7) Bike 17.6 km
   Swim ? km
   Run 4.4 km
   Total 23 km
   ☐ km

8) Bike 19.8 km
   Swim 700 m
   Run ? km
   Total 25 km
   ☐ km

9) Bike 21.3 km
   Swim 900 m
   Run ? km
   Total 26 km
   ☐ km

10) Bike 17.2 km
    Swim 600 m
    Run ? km
    Total 22 km
    ☐ km

Today I scored ☐ out of 10.

Week 6 — Day 4

Class 5 are cooking pancakes. Use the recipe to calculate the quantities they need.

Makes 10
200 ml milk
300 g flour

How much milk is needed to make 20 pancakes?

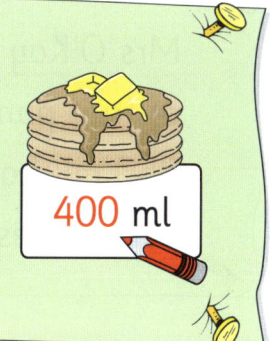

400 ml

1. Makes 8 — 300 ml milk, 275 g flour. How much milk is needed to make 24 pancakes? ____ ml

2. Makes 5 — 100 g flour, 2 eggs. How much flour is needed to make 30 pancakes? ____ g

3. Makes 20 — 500 ml milk, 80 g butter. How much milk is needed to make 4 pancakes? ____ ml

4. Makes 15 — 0.5 kg flour, 8 eggs. How much flour is needed to make 60 pancakes? ____ kg

5. Makes 40 — 800 ml milk, 8 eggs. How much milk is needed to make 10 pancakes? ____ ml

6. Makes 24 — 300 g flour, 40 g butter. How much flour is needed to make 8 pancakes? ____ g

7. Makes 30 — 60 g butter, 4 eggs. How much butter is needed to make 120 pancakes? ____ g

8. Makes 12 — 500 ml milk, 30 g flour. How much milk is needed to make 30 pancakes? ____ l

Today I scored ____ out of 8.

Week 6 — Day 5

Mrs O'Kay has made some jugs of fruit punch. If one glass holds 250 ml, how many full glasses of punch does the jug contain?

1. 1.25 l jug filled to 0.50

2. 1.25 l jug filled to 1.00

3. 2.5 l jug filled to 2.0

4. 2.5 l jug filled to 1.5

5. 2.5 l jug filled to 1.75

6. 5 l jug filled to 3

7. 1.0 l jug filled to 0.5

8. 2.5 l jug filled to 2.25

Today I scored ☐ out of 8.

Week 7 — Day 1

Write the mixed number as an improper fraction.

$3\frac{3}{4}$ = $\frac{15}{4}$

1) $4\frac{1}{2}$ =

2) $5\frac{2}{3}$ =

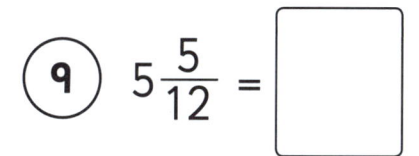

3) $6\frac{1}{5}$ =

4) $8\frac{3}{10}$ =

5) $4\frac{2}{7}$ =

6) $10\frac{1}{6}$ =

7) $1\frac{8}{11}$ =

8) $5\frac{7}{9}$ =

9) $5\frac{5}{12}$ =

10) $7\frac{5}{6}$ =

11) $6\frac{3}{8}$ =

12) $8\frac{5}{9}$ =

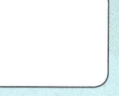

Today I scored ☐ out of 12.

Week 7 — Day 2

Circle the number that is the best estimate for the calculation in the box.

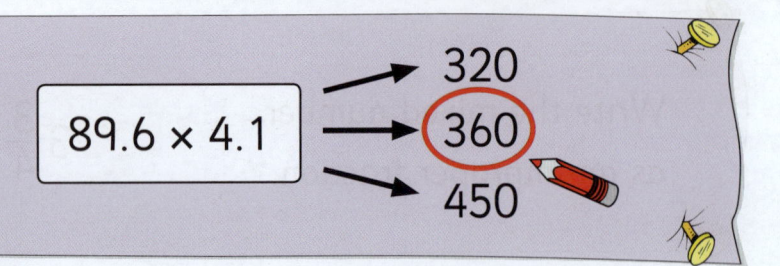

89.6 × 4.1 → 320 / **360** / 450

1) 241 ÷ 2.9 → 120 / 60 / 80

2) 9.5 × 252 → 2500 / 4750 / 3200

3) 6.8 × 10.2 → 70 / 60 / 75

4) 980 ÷ 4.88 → 250 / 300 / 200

5) 55.7 ÷ 6.8 → 5 / 8 / 10

6) 202 × 13.1 → 2100 / 2000 / 2600

7) 5012 ÷ 24.8 → 200 / 250 / 280

8) 490.4 ÷ 7.1 → 80 / 70 / 60

9) 30.2 × 11.8 → 300 / 320 / 360

10) 90.9 × 2.8 → 300 / 270 / 182

11) 16.2 × 197 → 3200 / 4000 / 2000

12) 357 ÷ 5.8 → 50 / 60 / 70

Today I scored ☐ out of 12.

Week 7 — Day 3

A class had a vote to choose an animal as their class mascot. The graph shows the number of votes for each animal. Use the graph to answer the question.

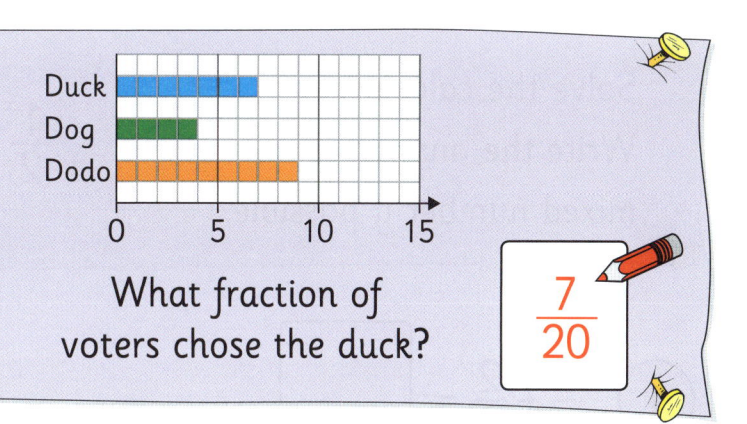

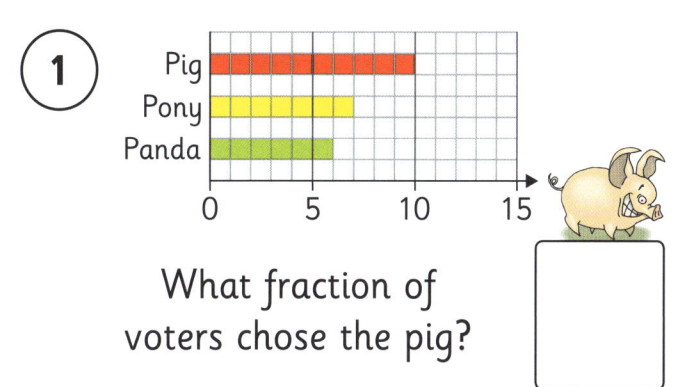

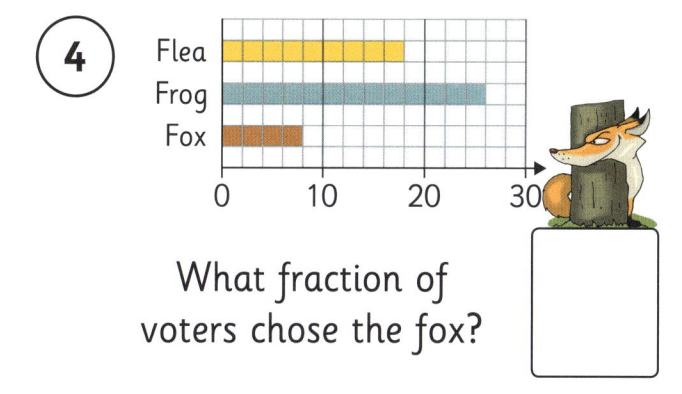

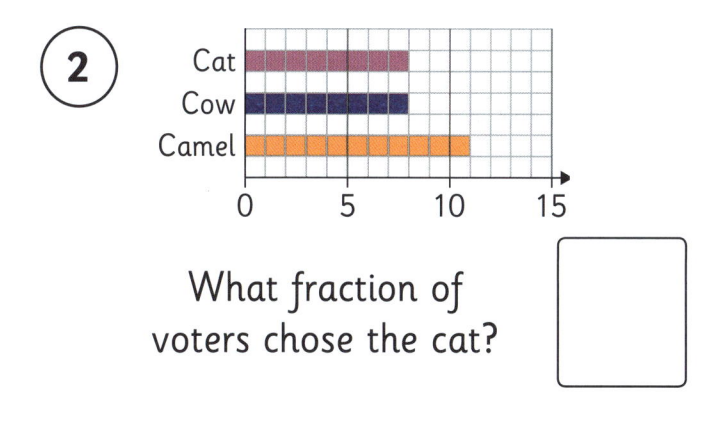

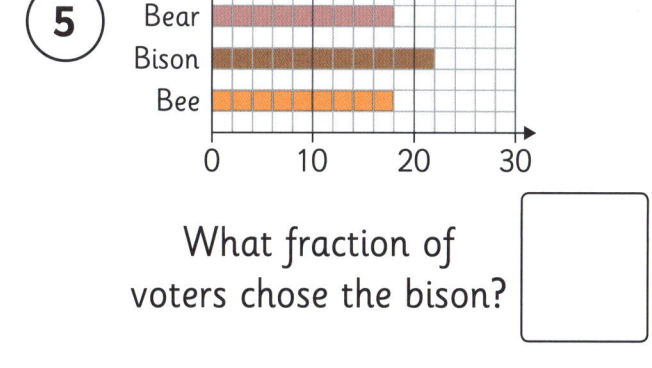

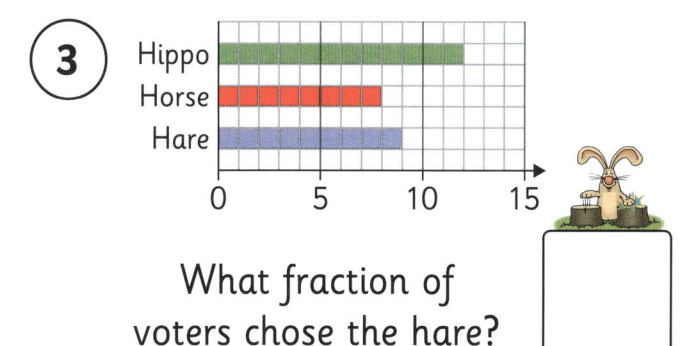

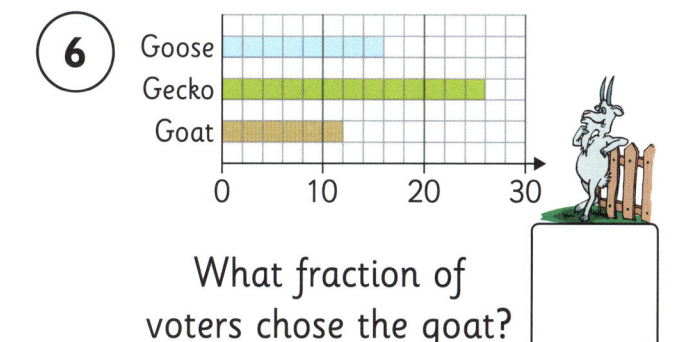

What fraction of voters chose the duck? $\frac{7}{20}$

1 What fraction of voters chose the pig?

2 What fraction of voters chose the cat?

3 What fraction of voters chose the hare?

4 What fraction of voters chose the fox?

5 What fraction of voters chose the bison?

6 What fraction of voters chose the goat?

Today I scored ☐ out of 6.

Week 7 — Day 4

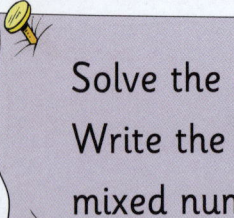

Solve the calculation. Write the answer as a mixed number if possible.

$\frac{1}{2} + \frac{7}{8} = \boxed{1\frac{3}{8}}$

1) $\frac{1}{6} + \frac{2}{3} = \boxed{}$

2) $\frac{7}{10} - \frac{2}{5} = \boxed{}$

3) $\frac{2}{3} + \frac{1}{12} = \boxed{}$

4) $\frac{3}{4} + \frac{3}{8} = \boxed{}$

5) $\frac{8}{9} - \frac{1}{3} = \boxed{}$

6) $\frac{71}{100} + \frac{11}{20} = \boxed{}$

7) $\frac{43}{50} - \frac{1}{2} = \boxed{}$

8) $\frac{7}{16} + \frac{3}{4} = \boxed{}$

9) $\frac{5}{6} - \frac{7}{36} = \boxed{}$

10) $\frac{3}{7} + \frac{31}{35} = \boxed{}$

11) $\frac{11}{18} - \frac{1}{3} = \boxed{}$

12) $\frac{3}{4} - \frac{13}{100} = \boxed{}$

Today I scored ☐ out of 12.

Week 7 — Day 5

Cathy painted a wall using 6 vertical stripes. She painted 3 red stripes, 2 yellow stripes and 1 pink stripe. Find the width of the pink stripe in cm.

The wall is 2 m wide.
Each red stripe is 0.4 m wide.
Each yellow stripe is 25 cm wide.

The pink stripe is **30** cm wide.

1) The wall is 3 m wide.
Each red stripe is 50 cm wide.
Each yellow stripe is 40 cm wide.

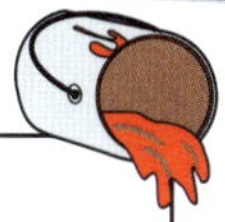

The pink stripe is ____ cm wide.

2) The wall is 2.5 m wide.
Each red stripe is 33 cm wide.
Each yellow stripe is 22 cm wide.

The pink stripe is ____ cm wide.

3) The wall is 240 cm wide.
Each red stripe is 0.3 m wide.
Each yellow stripe is 0.5 m wide.

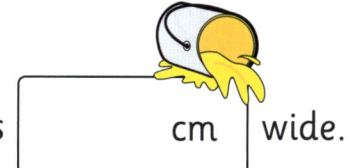

The pink stripe is ____ cm wide.

4) The wall is 4.3 m wide.
Each red stripe is 72 cm wide.
Each yellow stripe is 0.84 m wide.

The pink stripe is ____ cm wide.

5) The wall is 545 cm wide.
Each red stripe is 1.25 m wide.
Each yellow stripe is 0.53 m wide.

The pink stripe is ____ cm wide.

6) The wall is 4.85 m wide.
Each red stripe is 55 cm wide.
Each yellow stripe is 0.91 m wide.

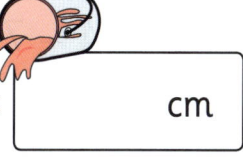

The pink stripe is ____ cm wide.

Today I scored ____ out of 6.

Week 8 — Day 1

Solve the calculation.   14 438 + 4261 = 18 699

1) 66 423 + 3166 =

2) 50 500 − 6050 =

3) 32 198 + 8912 =

4) 95 386 − 1156 =

5) 49 773 + 6621 =

6) 17 844 − 7845 =

7) 32 932 + 8282 =

8) 44 756 − 7878 =

9) 71 318 + 2993 =

10) 48 638 − 5749 =

11) 59 726 + 5697 =

12) 11 243 − 9775 =

Today I scored ☐ out of 12.

Week 8 — Day 2

Work out the missing angle in the diagram. The diagrams on this page are not drawn to scale.

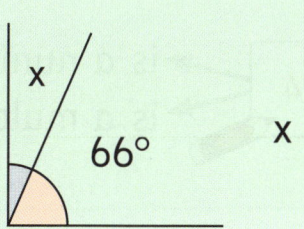

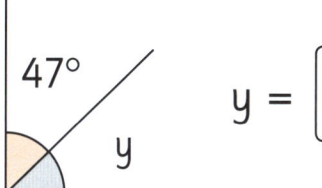

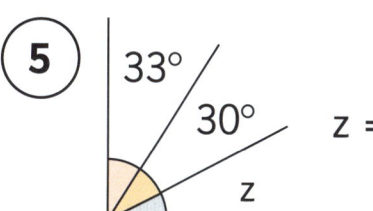

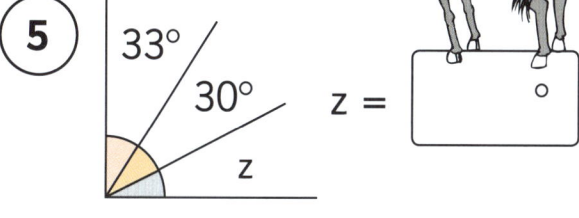

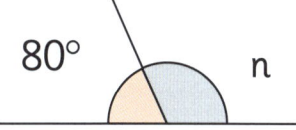

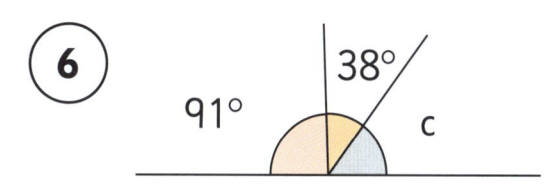

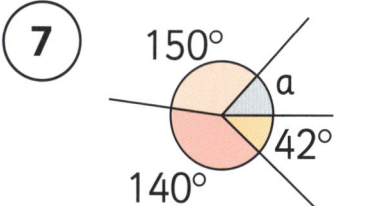

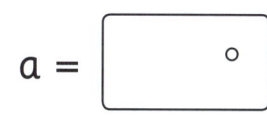

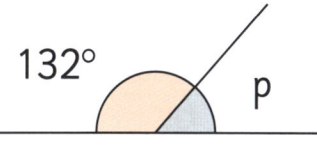

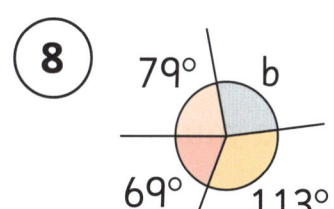

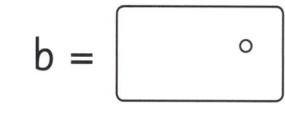

Example: x with 66°, x = 24°

1) 47°, y =
2) 80°, n =
3) 74°, m =
4) 132°, p =
5) 33°, 30°, z =
6) 91°, 38°, c =
7) 150°, 140°, 42°, a =
8) 79°, 69°, 113°, b =

Today I scored ☐ out of 8.

Week 8 — Day 3

Fill in the missing number. **24** → is a number between 20 and 30.
→ is a multiple of 4 and a multiple of 6.

1. ☐ → is a number between 15 and 22.
   → is a multiple of 3 and a multiple of 6.

2. ☐ → is a number between 40 and 55.
   → is a multiple of 5 and a multiple of 3.

3. ☐ → is a number between 40 and 50.
   → is a multiple of 6 and a multiple of 4.

4. ☐ → is a number between 20 and 50.
   → is a multiple of 11 and a multiple 4.

5. ☐ → is a number between 60 and 100.
   → is a multiple of 7 and a multiple of 12.

6. ☐ → is a number between 100 and 120.
   → is a multiple of 12 and a multiple of 9.

7. ☐ → is a number between 60 and 80.
   → is a multiple of 8 and a multiple of 6.

8. ☐ → is a number between 100 and 140.
   → is a multiple of 11 and a multiple of 4.

Today I scored ☐ out of 8.

Week 8 — Day 4

Craig puts a number into the number machine. What is his answer?

22 → ×2 → +250 → round to the nearest 10 → 290

1) 33 → ×4 → +189 → round to the nearest 10 → ☐

2) 46 → ×6 → +115 → round to the nearest 100 → ☐

3) 87 → ×5 → +349 → round to the nearest 10 → ☐

4) 91 → ×9 → +232 → round to the nearest 100 → ☐

5) 59 → ×3 → +684 → round to the nearest 10 → ☐

6) 69 → ×7 → +287 → round to the nearest 100 → ☐

7) 76 → ×9 → −439 → round to the nearest 10 → ☐

8) 89 → ×8 → −569 → round to the nearest 10 → ☐

Today I scored ☐ out of 8.

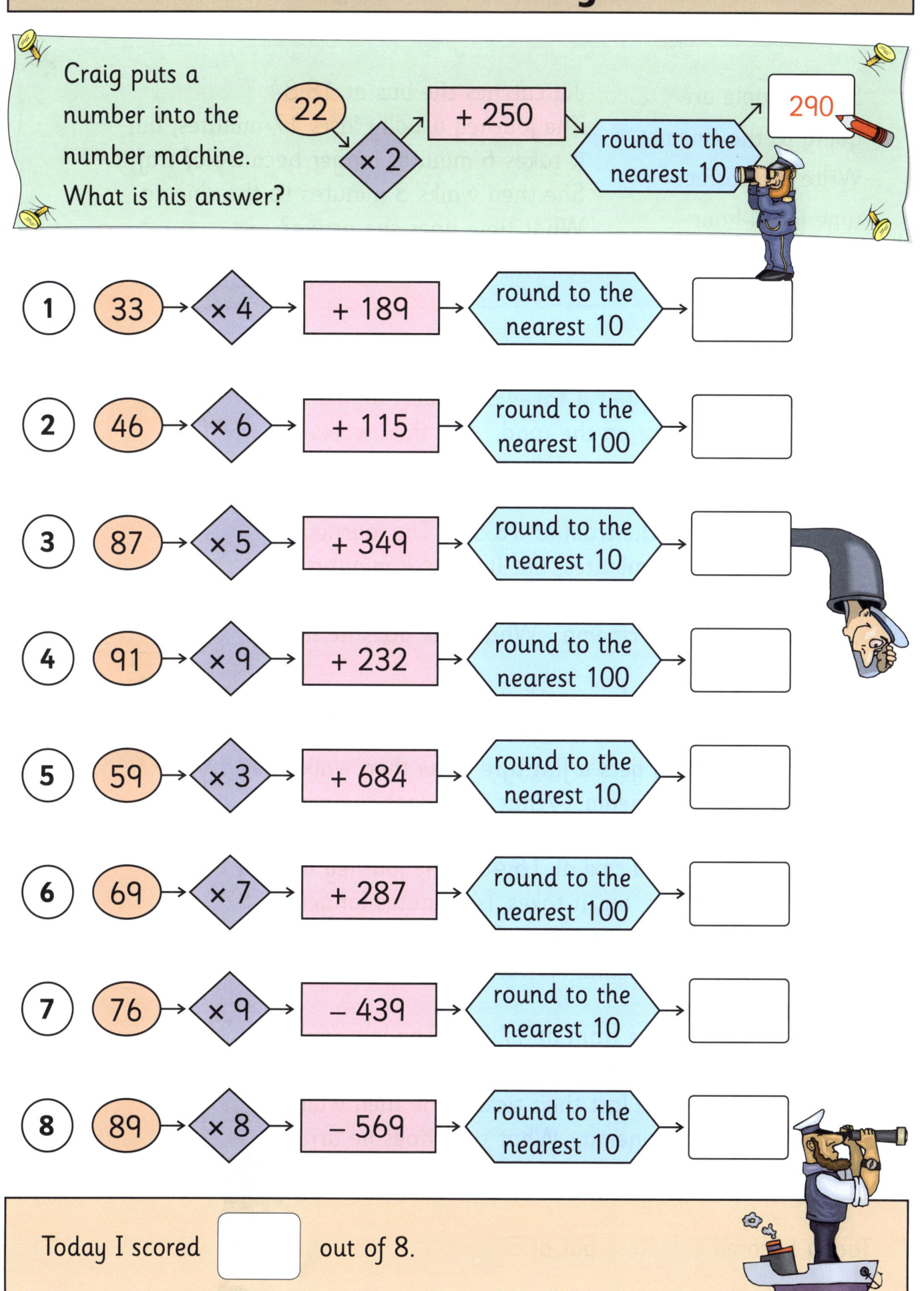

Week 8 — Day 5

Some people are going to the cinema. Write the correct time in 24-hour clock format.

Jill catches the bus at 18:34. The journey usually lasts 17 minutes, but it takes 6 minutes longer because of traffic. She then walks 3 minutes to the cinema. What time does she arrive?

19:00

1) Vicky catches the bus at 17:12. The journey usually lasts 29 minutes, but it takes 3 minutes longer because cows are on the road. She then walks 15 minutes to the cinema. What time does she arrive?

2) Robbie catches the train at 18:56. The journey usually lasts 11 minutes, but it takes 4 minutes longer because the track is flooded. He then walks 9 minutes to the cinema. What time does he arrive?

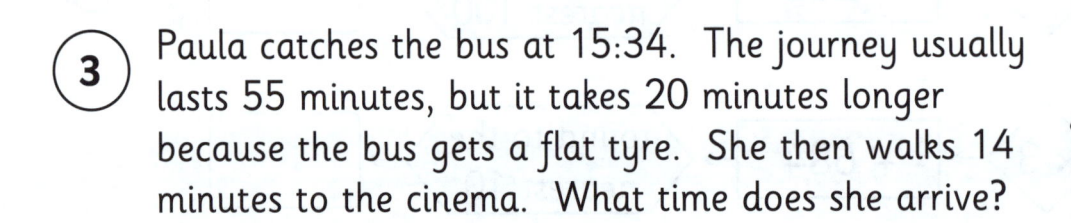

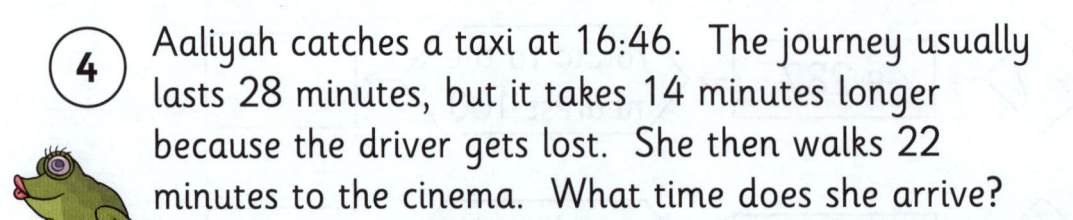

3) Paula catches the bus at 15:34. The journey usually lasts 55 minutes, but it takes 20 minutes longer because the bus gets a flat tyre. She then walks 14 minutes to the cinema. What time does she arrive?

4) Aaliyah catches a taxi at 16:46. The journey usually lasts 28 minutes, but it takes 14 minutes longer because the driver gets lost. She then walks 22 minutes to the cinema. What time does she arrive?

5) Marty catches the tram at 17:58. The journey usually lasts 19 minutes, but it takes 8 minutes longer because someone lost their ticket. He then walks 27 minutes to the cinema. What time does he arrive?

Today I scored ☐ out of 5.

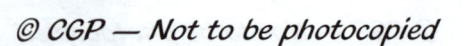

Year 5 Maths — Spring Term

Week 9 — Day 1

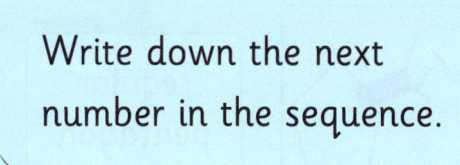

Write down the next number in the sequence.

13 413, 113 413, 213 413, ...

313 413

1) 15 445, 15 345, 15 245, ...

2) 5202, 5210, 5218, ...

3) 48 265, 48 270, 48 275, ...

4) 781 123, 881 123, 981 123, ...

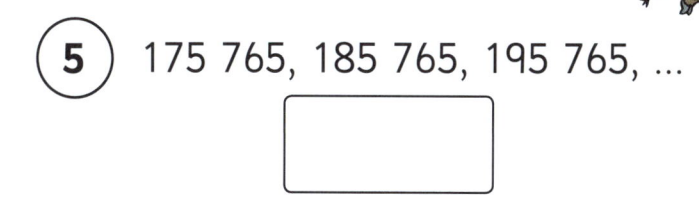

5) 175 765, 185 765, 195 765, ...

6) 26 446, 26 440, 26 434, ...

7) 1385, 1394, 1403, ...

8) 97 139, 98 139, 99 139, ...

9) 27 341, 27 361, 27 381, ...

10) 65 273, 65 269, 65 265, ...

11) 34 589, 34 789, 34 989, ...

12) 89 323, 94 323, 99 323, ...

Today I scored ☐ out of 12.

Week 9 — Day 2

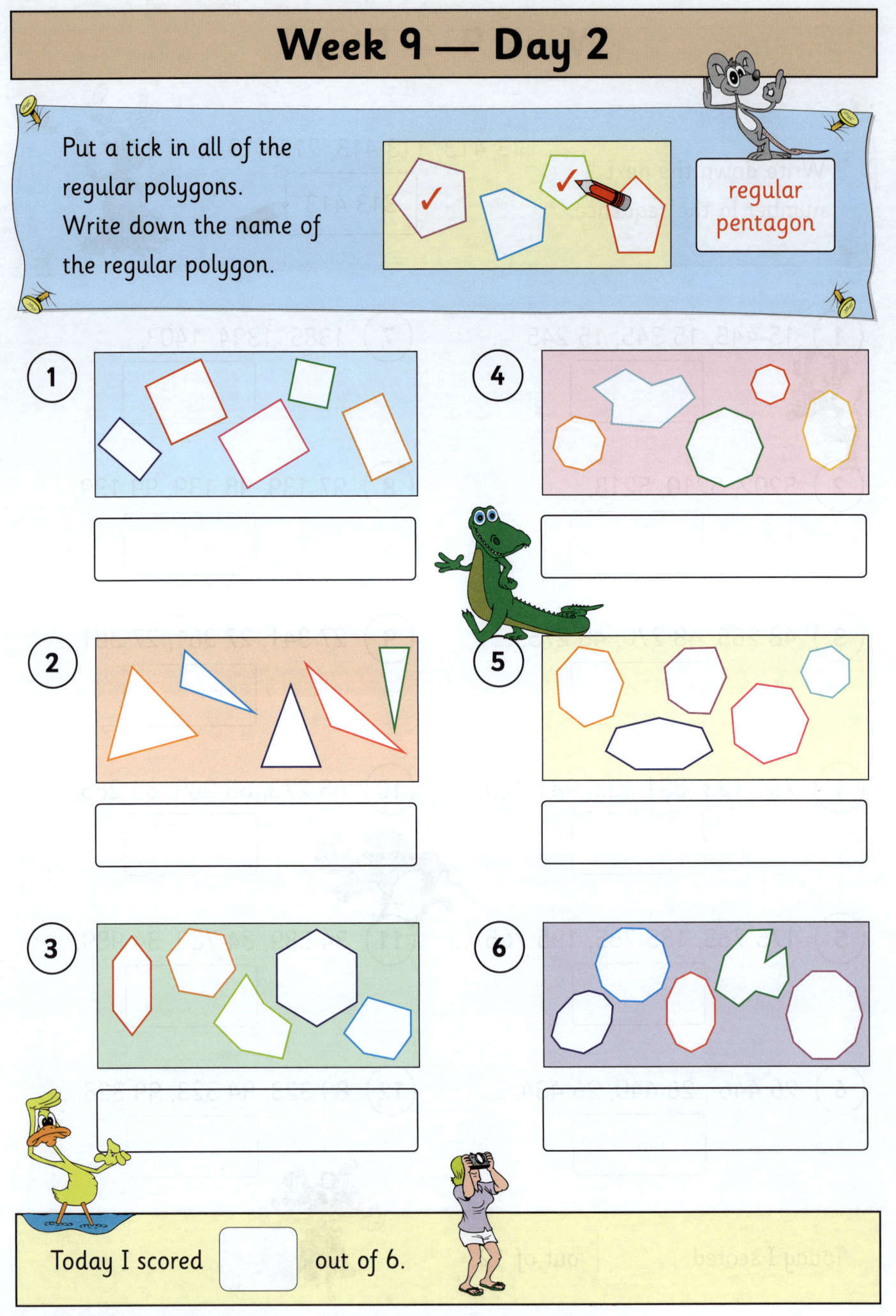

Put a tick in all of the regular polygons.
Write down the name of the regular polygon.

regular pentagon

1.

2.

3.

4.

5.

6.

Today I scored ☐ out of 6.

Year 5 Maths — Spring Term

Week 9 — Day 3

Find the length of the distance labelled A. The shapes are not drawn to scale.

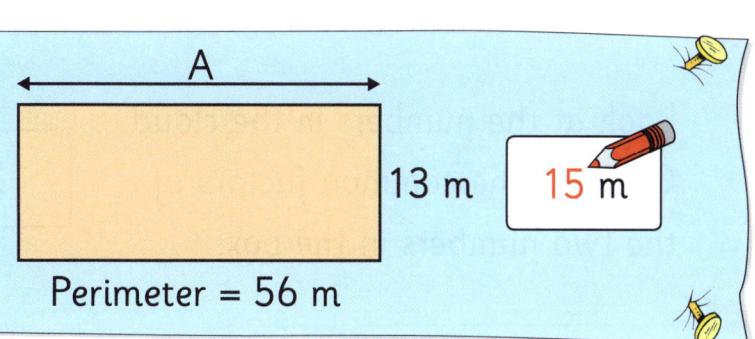

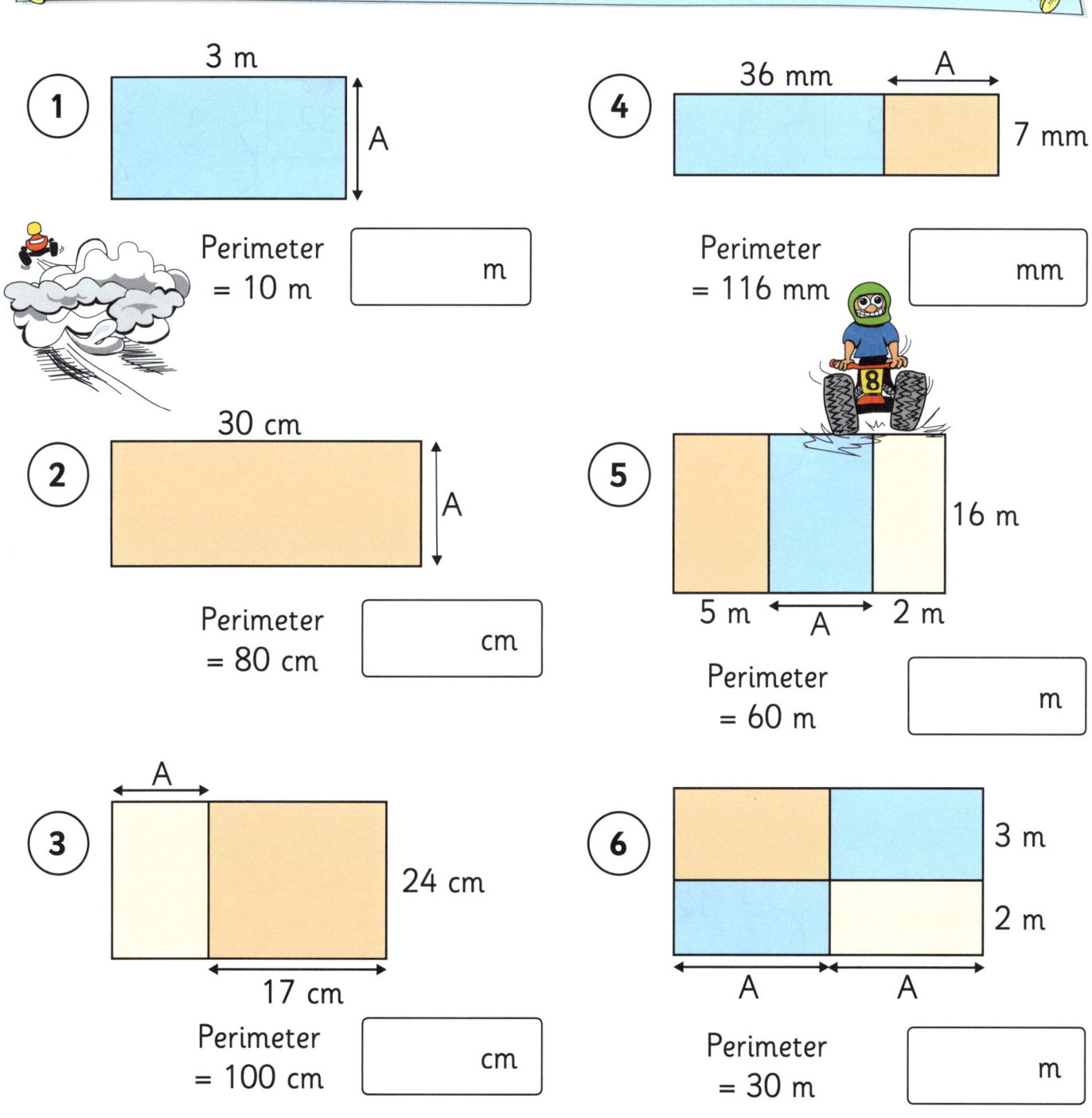

Example: Rectangle with A on top, 13 m on side, Perimeter = 56 m, Answer: **15 m**

1 Rectangle, 3 m top, A side, Perimeter = 10 m → ☐ m

2 Rectangle, 30 cm top, A side, Perimeter = 80 cm → ☐ cm

3 Rectangle split into two parts, A on top-left, 24 cm side, 17 cm bottom-right, Perimeter = 100 cm → ☐ cm

4 Rectangle split into two parts, 36 mm left, A right, 7 mm side, Perimeter = 116 mm → ☐ mm

5 Rectangle split into three parts, 5 m, A, 2 m along bottom, 16 m side, Perimeter = 60 m → ☐ m

6 Rectangle split into four parts, 3 m and 2 m on right side, A and A along bottom, Perimeter = 30 m → ☐ m

Today I scored ☐ out of 6.

Week 9 — Day 4

Look at the numbers in the cloud. Circle all the common factors of the two numbers in the box.

12, 16

Cloud: (2), 6, 3, 8, 9, (4)

1) 9, 15 — Cloud: 2, 6, 3, 8, 9, 4

2) 30, 40 — Cloud: 2, 8, 3, 5, 4, 7

3) 14, 21 — Cloud: 21, 3, 9, 8, 7, 4

4) 18, 24 — Cloud: 12, 6, 3, 8, 5, 4

5) 24, 32 — Cloud: 2, 16, 3, 8, 9, 4

6) 25, 75 — Cloud: 15, 5, 3, 10, 50, 9

7) 18, 27 — Cloud: 2, 1, 3, 8, 6, 9

8) 32, 64 — Cloud: 2, 6, 8, 1, 12, 16

Today I scored ☐ out of 8.

Week 9 — Day 5

Find the size of the angle marked Z. The shapes are not drawn to scale.

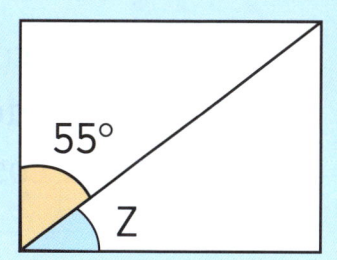

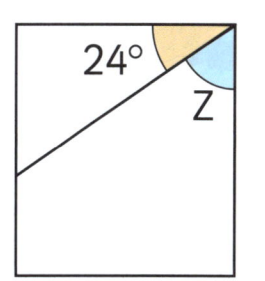

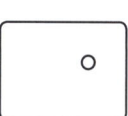

55° Z → **35°**

1. 60°, Z → ☐°

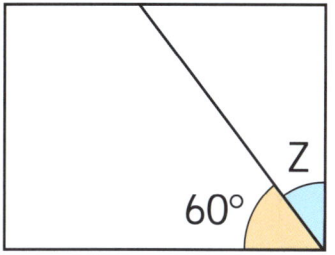

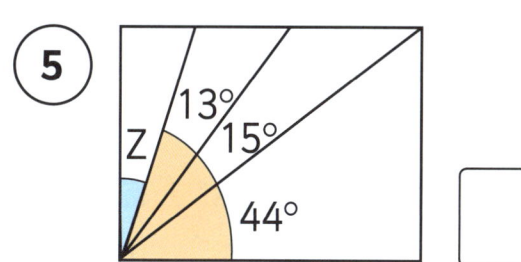

2. 24°, Z → ☐°

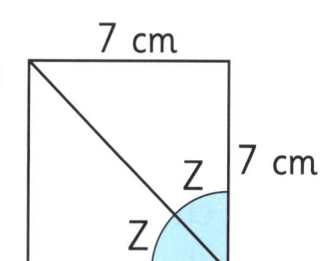

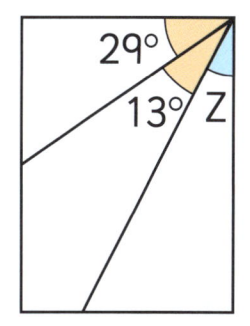

3. 29°, 13°, Z → ☐°

4. 21°, Z, 33° → ☐°

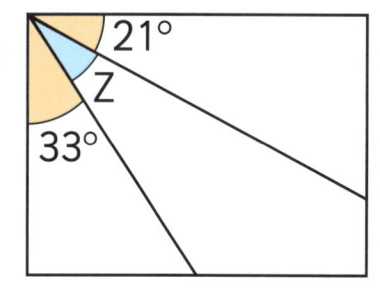

5. 13°, 15°, 44°, Z → ☐°

6. 7 cm, 7 cm, Z, Z → ☐°

7. 49°, 72°, Z → ☐°

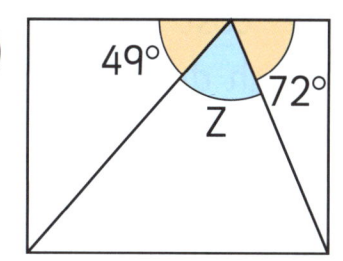

8. 67°, 55°, Z → ☐°

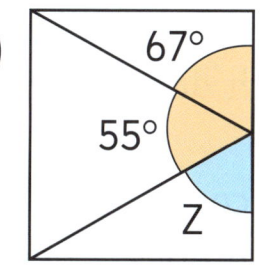

Today I scored ☐ out of 8.

Week 10 — Day 1

Fill in the answer.

6 bananas cost £1.20. How much does 1 banana cost? **20** p

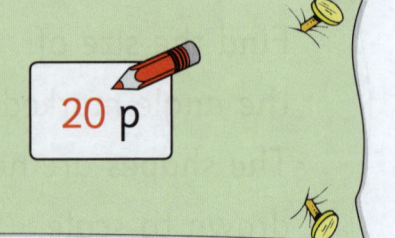

1. 8 tomatoes cost £0.72. How much does 1 tomato cost? ☐ p

2. 3 cucumbers cost £1.56. How much does 1 cucumber cost? ☐ p

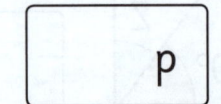

3. 6 carrots cost £1.80. How much does 1 carrot cost? ☐ p

4. 4 boxes of cherries cost £3.60. How much does 1 box cost? ☐ p

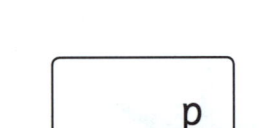

5. 6 apples cost £1.38. How much does 1 apple cost? ☐ p

6. 9 pears cost £1.17. How much does 1 pear cost? ☐ p

7. 9 oranges cost £2.34. How much does 1 orange cost? ☐ p

8. 7 onions cost £3.85. How much does 1 onion cost? ☐ p

Today I scored ☐ out of 8.

Year 5 Maths — Spring Term

Week 10 — Day 2

Bina is making shapes using identical rectangular tiles.
Find the perimeter of the shape.
The shapes are not drawn to scale.

6 cm
9 cm
48 cm

1) 4.6 cm, 6 cm — ___ cm

2) 6.3 cm, 9.6 cm — ___ cm

3) 6.5 cm, 7.6 cm — ___ cm

4) 2.5 cm, 8 cm — ___ cm

5) 2.7 cm, 5.1 cm — ___ cm

6) 13 cm, 11 cm — ___ cm

7) 7 cm, 4 cm — ___ cm

8) 5.6 cm, 9.2 cm — ___ cm

Today I scored ☐ out of 8.

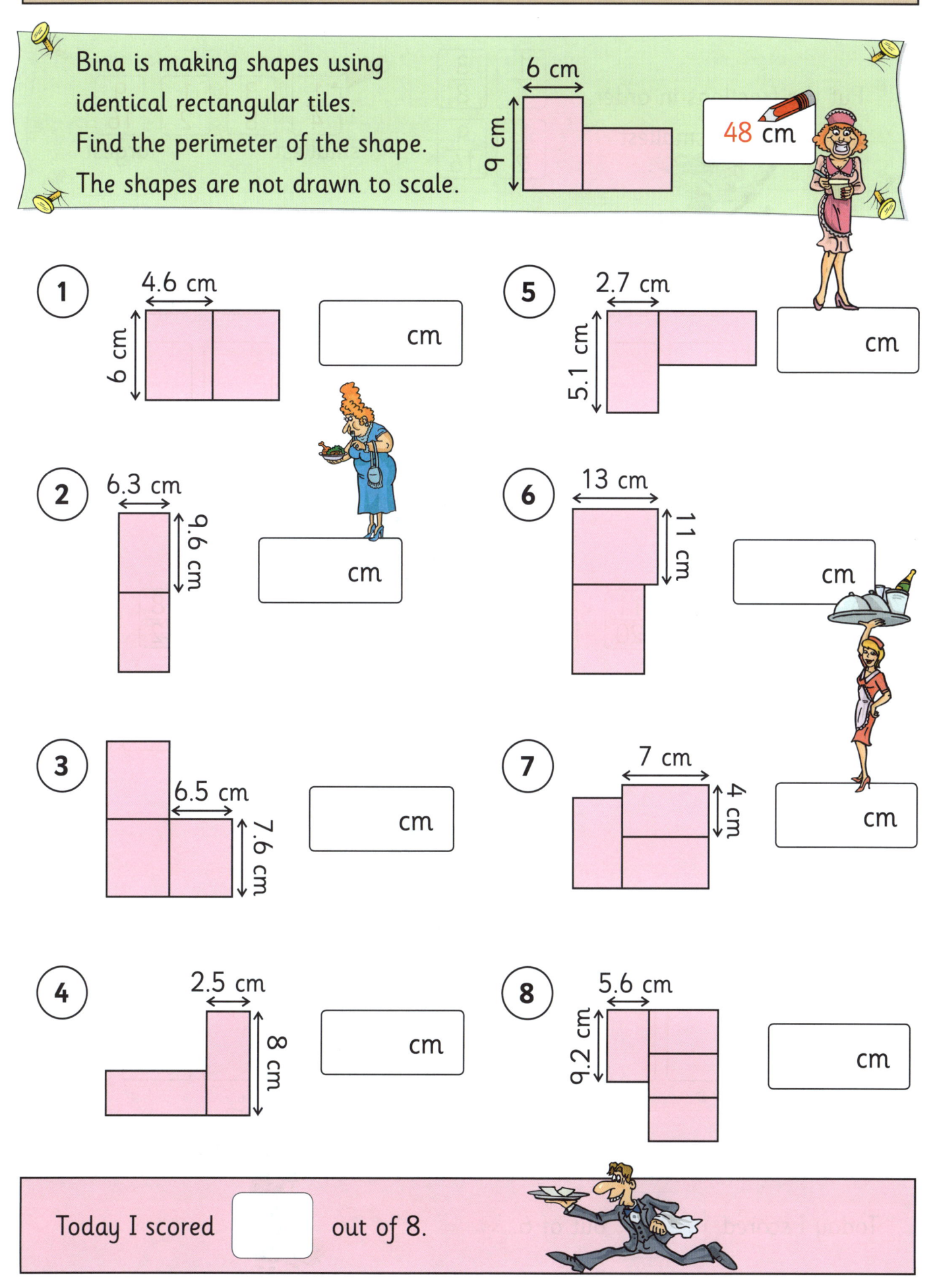

Week 10 — Day 3

Put the fractions in order. Start with the smallest.

$\frac{1}{4}$ $\frac{3}{8}$ $\frac{1}{2}$ $\frac{9}{16}$

$\frac{1}{4}$ $\frac{3}{8}$ $\frac{1}{2}$ $\frac{9}{16}$
smallest → largest

1) $\frac{2}{10}$ $\frac{11}{15}$ $\frac{4}{5}$ $\frac{12}{30}$

smallest → largest

4) $\frac{2}{5}$ $\frac{11}{30}$ $\frac{12}{15}$ $\frac{25}{60}$

smallest → largest

2) $\frac{1}{2}$ $\frac{23}{40}$ $\frac{11}{20}$ $\frac{6}{10}$

smallest → largest

5) $\frac{2}{12}$ $\frac{14}{24}$ $\frac{18}{72}$ $\frac{1}{3}$

smallest → largest

3) $\frac{2}{3}$ $\frac{16}{18}$ $\frac{29}{36}$ $\frac{7}{9}$

smallest → largest

6) $\frac{5}{8}$ $\frac{48}{64}$ $\frac{19}{32}$ $\frac{11}{16}$

smallest → largest

Today I scored ☐ out of 6.

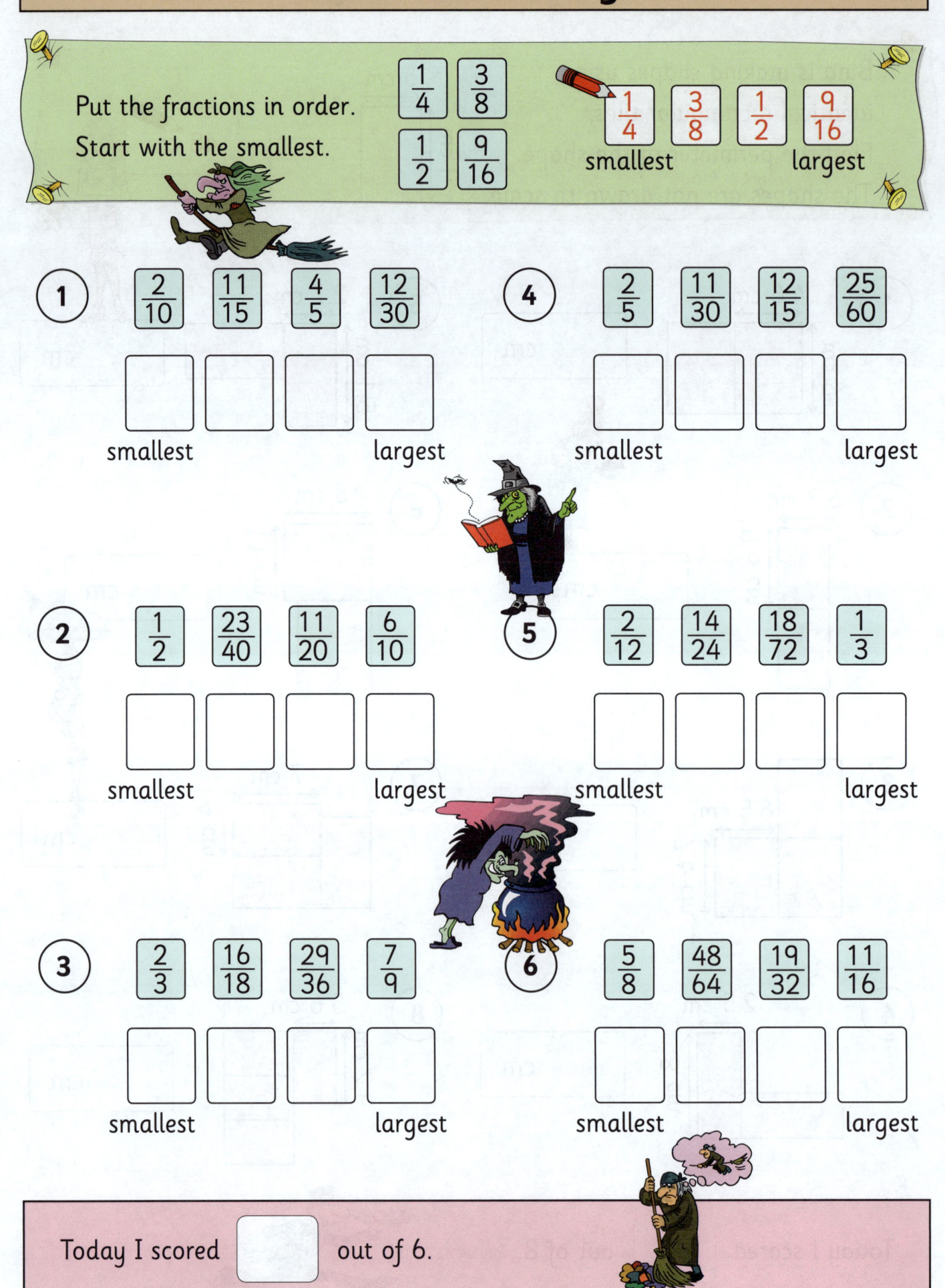

Week 10 — Day 4

Work out the area of the rectangle. The rectangles are not drawn to scale.

21 cm × 3 cm = **63** cm²

1) 11 cm × 6 cm = ☐ cm²

2) 10 cm × 13 cm = ☐ cm²

3) 18 cm × 5 cm = ☐ cm²

4) 14 cm × 8 cm = ☐ cm²

5) 22 cm × 7 cm = ☐ cm²

6) 19 cm × 9 cm = ☐ cm²

7) 25 cm × 12 cm = ☐ cm²

8) 26 cm × 17 cm = ☐ cm²

Today I scored ☐ out of 8.

Week 10 — Day 5

Fill in the correct number.

Each week, a shop sells 112 colas and 87 lemonades. How many more colas are sold in 4 weeks than lemonades?

100 colas

1. Each week, a shop sells 44 plates and 18 bowls. How many more plates are sold in 6 weeks than bowls?

☐ plates

2. Each week, a shop sells 193 shirts and 57 jackets. How many more shirts are sold in 5 weeks than jackets?

☐ shirts

3. Each week, a shop sells 435 white loaves and 231 brown loaves. How many more white loaves are sold in 3 weeks than brown loaves?

☐ white loaves

4. Each week, a shop sells 248 toilet rolls and 31 toilet brushes. How many more toilet rolls are sold in 7 weeks than toilet brushes?

☐ toilet rolls

5. Each week, a shop sells 269 eggs and 93 bags of flour. How many more eggs are sold in 8 weeks than bags of flour?

☐ eggs

6. Each week, a shop sells 247 newspapers and 159 magazines. How many more newspapers are sold in 9 weeks than magazines?

☐ newspapers

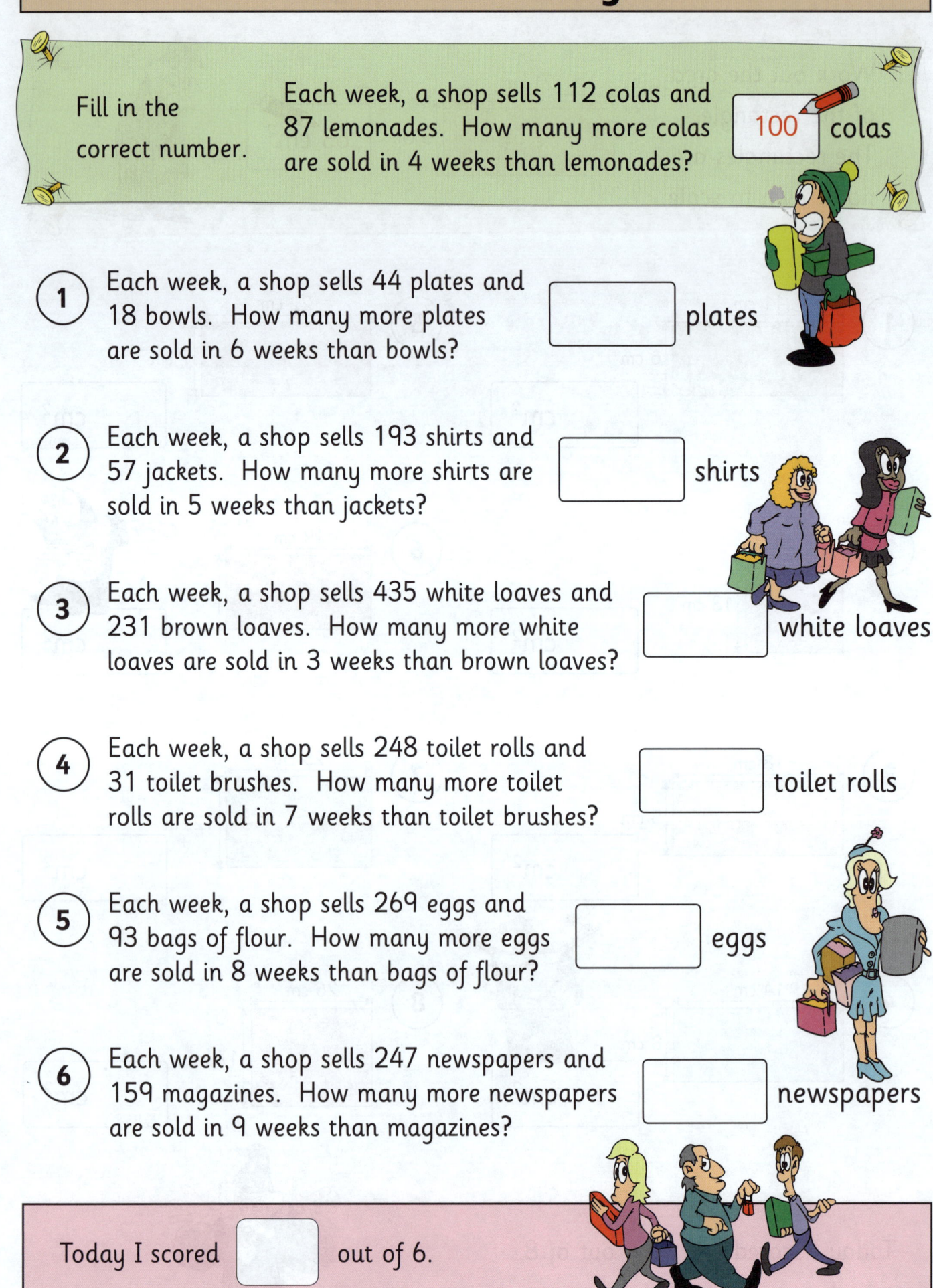

Today I scored ☐ out of 6.

Week 11 — Day 1

Circle the name of the 3D shape that the net will fold up to make.

Cube

1.

2.

3.

4.

5.

6.

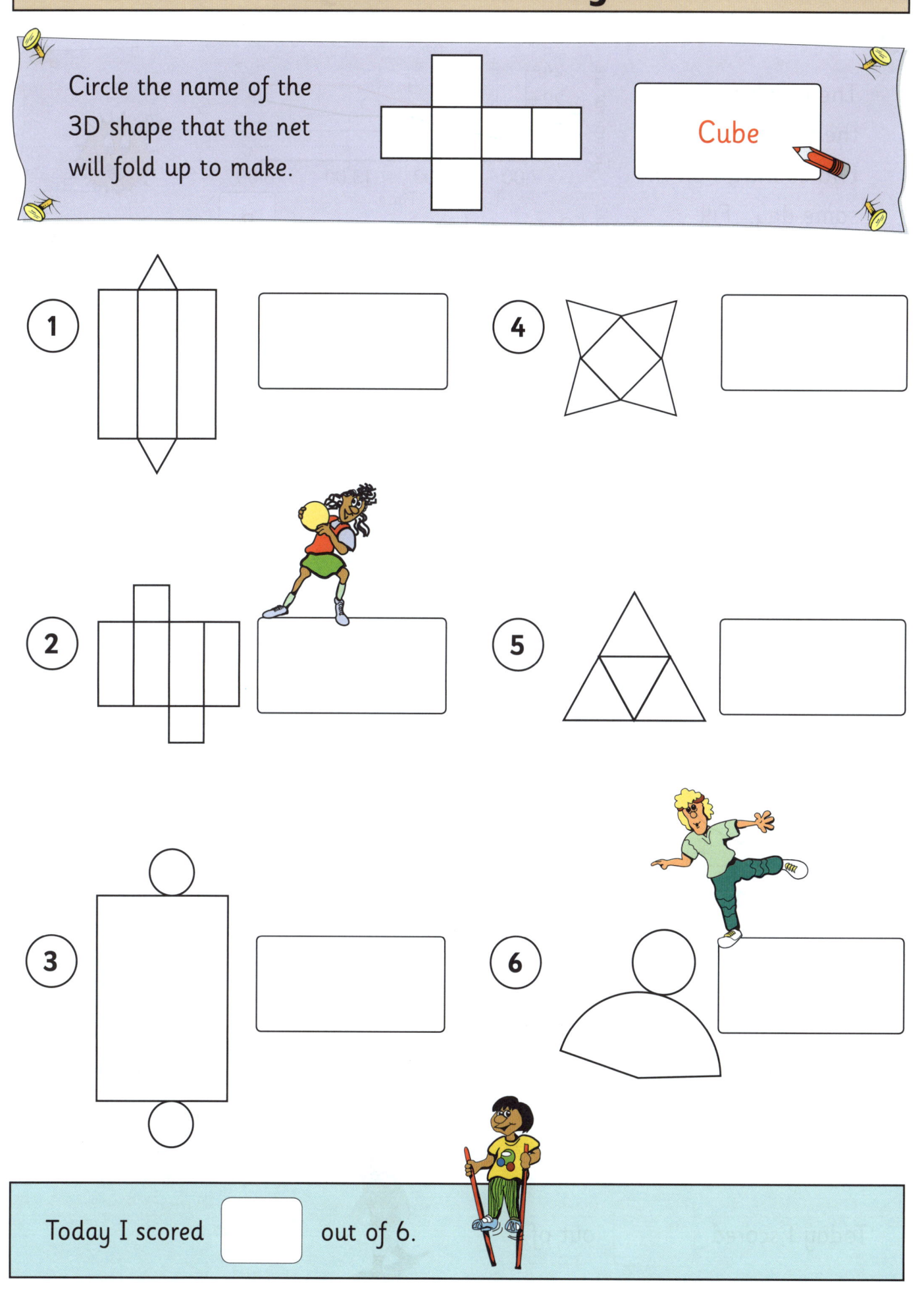

Today I scored ☐ out of 6.

Week 11 — Day 2

The graph shows the temperature in two countries on the same day. Fill in the answers.

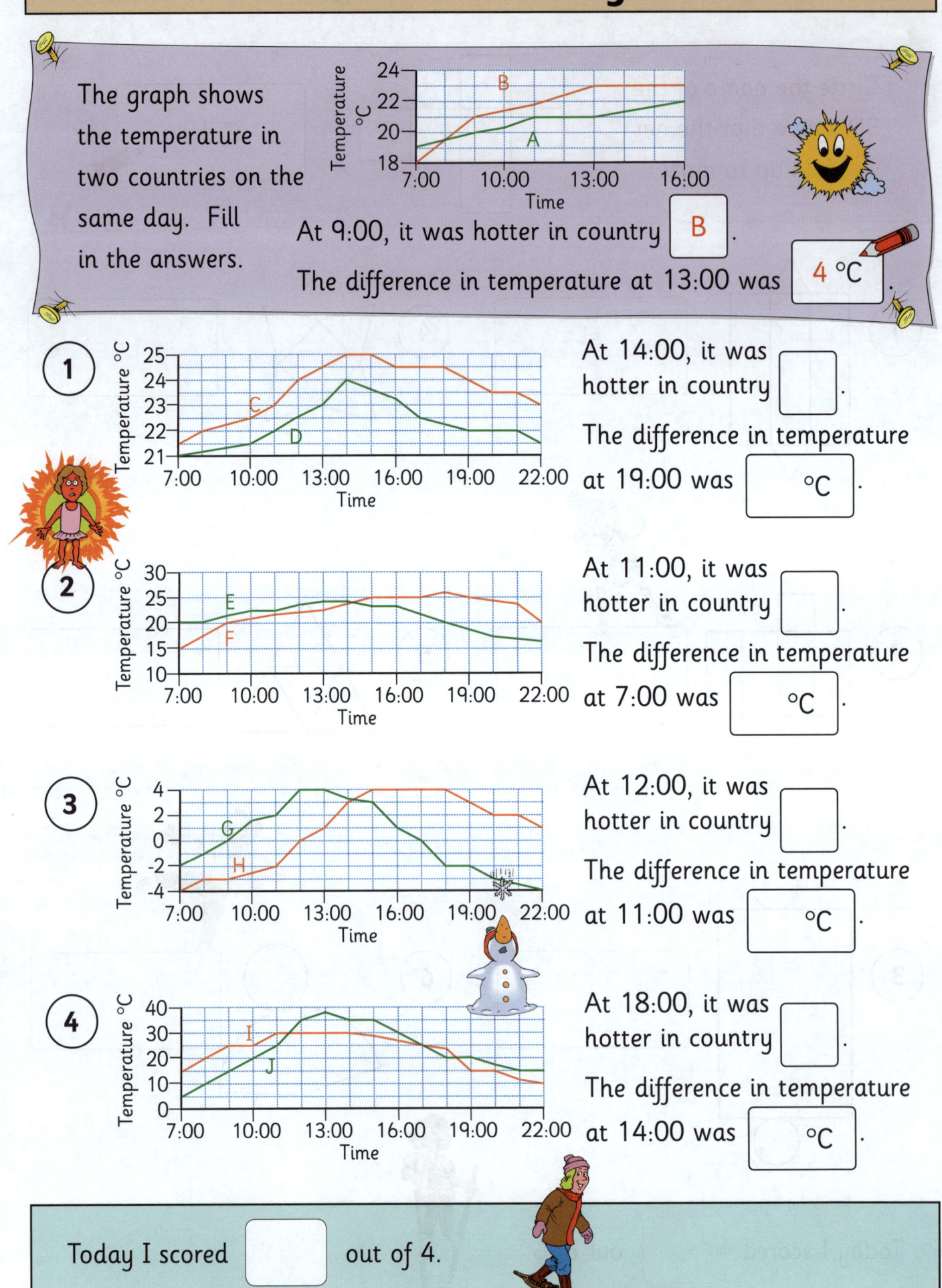

At 9:00, it was hotter in country [B].

The difference in temperature at 13:00 was [4] °C.

1 At 14:00, it was hotter in country [ ].

The difference in temperature at 19:00 was [ ] °C.

2 At 11:00, it was hotter in country [ ].

The difference in temperature at 7:00 was [ ] °C.

3 At 12:00, it was hotter in country [ ].

The difference in temperature at 11:00 was [ ] °C.

4 At 18:00, it was hotter in country [ ].

The difference in temperature at 14:00 was [ ] °C.

Today I scored [ ] out of 4.

Year 5 Maths — Spring Term

Week 11 — Day 3

Complete the calculation.   800 000 − 75 000 = **725 000**

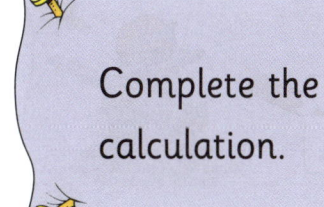

1) 15 300 + 2600 =

2) 17 420 + 1400 =

3) 21 243 + 8500 =

4) 1 350 000 + 240 000 =

5) 2 780 000 + 510 000 =

6) 4 921 000 + 232 000 =

7) 900 000 − 25 000 =

8) 96 500 − 25 000 =

9) 687 000 − 1 500 =

10) 454 000 − 2 300 =

11) 1 394 000 − 75 000 =

12) 2 472 000 − 154 000 =

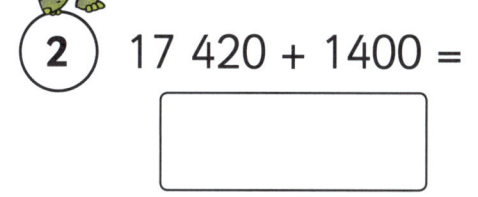

Today I scored ☐ out of 12.

Week 11 — Day 4

Each cube has a volume of 1 cm³. Work out the volume of the shape.

Example: 6 cm³

1) ___ cm³

2) ___ cm³

3) ___ cm³

4) ___ cm³

5) ___ cm³

6) ___ cm³

7) ___ cm³

8) ___ cm³

Today I scored ___ out of 8.

Week 11 — Day 5

Ava's sweet shop sells peppermints for 2p, lollies for 5p and chocolate bars for 10p. Work out how much money Ava makes.

On Sunday, Ava sells 370 peppermints, 530 lollies and 87 chocolate bars. How much money does she make?

£42.60

1 On Monday, Ava sells 210 peppermints, 220 lollies and 30 chocolate bars. How much money does she make?

£

2 On Tuesday, Ava sells 130 peppermints, 270 lollies and 42 chocolate bars. How much money does she make?

£

3 On Wednesday, Ava sells 280 peppermints, 370 lollies and 98 chocolate bars. How much money does she make?

£

4 On Thursday, Ava sells 642 peppermints, 232 lollies and 310 chocolate bars. How much money does she make?

£

5 On Friday, Ava sells 254 peppermints, 178 lollies and 120 chocolate bars. How much money does she make?

£

6 On Saturday, Ava sells 438 peppermints, 296 lollies and 250 chocolate bars. How much money does she make?

£

Today I scored ☐ out of 6.

Week 12 — Day 1

Round the decimal to one decimal place.   3.18 → 3.2

1) 7.74 → ☐
2) 0.83 → ☐
3) 6.09 → ☐
4) 4.45 → ☐
5) 8.66 → ☐
6) 5.02 → ☐

7) 0.433 → ☐
8) 1.234 → ☐
9) 3.555 → ☐
10) 9.99 → ☐
11) 6.899 → ☐
12) 0.548 → ☐

Today I scored ☐ out of 12.

Year 5 Maths — Spring Term

Week 12 — Day 2

Draw the angle in the pink box using a ruler and a protractor.

60°

1. 20°

2. 80°

3. 35°

4. 140°

5. 175°

6. 52°

7. 18°

8. 97°

9. 123°

10. 146°

Today I scored ☐ out of 10.

Week 12 — Day 3

Round the measurement to the nearest given unit.

A door is 204 cm tall. What is this to the nearest metre?

[2 m]

1. A bottle holds 750 ml. What is this to the nearest litre? [ ] l

2. A car weighs 1650.6 kg. What is this to the nearest kilogram? [ ] kg

3. A bag of sweets weighs 675 g. What is this to the nearest kilogram? [ ] kg

4. An ant weighs 0.005 g. What is this to the nearest gram? [ ] g

5. A bath holds 83 550 ml. What is this to the nearest litre? [ ] l

6. A building is 6446 cm tall. What is this to the nearest metre? [ ] m

7. A can holds 0.332 l. What is this to the nearest millilitre? [ ] ml

8. A lamppost is 3.834 m tall. What is this to the nearest centimetre? [ ] cm

Today I scored [ ] out of 8.

Week 12 — Day 4

Solve the calculation.

$$5 \overline{)41^17^2 4} = 834 \text{ r } 4$$

1) 3320 × 3 =

2) 4⟌5827 = ☐ r

3) 6741 × 5 =

4) 7⟌1992 = ☐ r

5) 2683 × 7 =

6) 8⟌5991 = ☐ r

7) 8173 × 6 =

8) 9⟌6184 = ☐ r

9) 4919 × 11 =

10) 7⟌9713 = ☐ r

Today I scored ☐ out of 10.

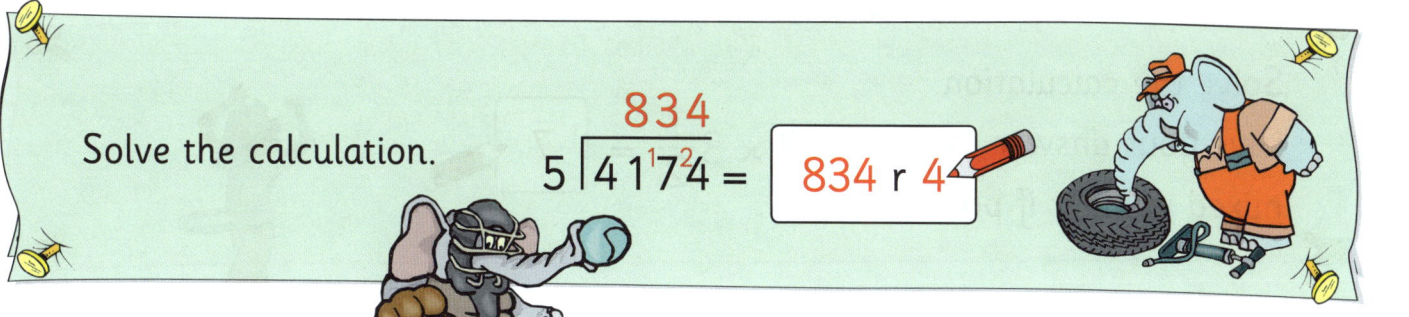

Week 12 — Day 5

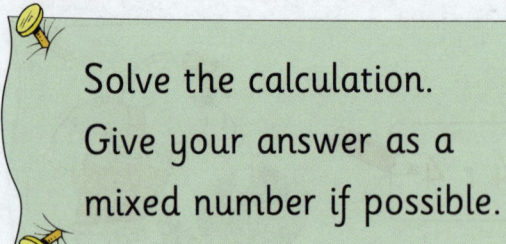

Solve the calculation. Give your answer as a mixed number if possible.

$2 \times 3\frac{1}{2} = \boxed{7}$

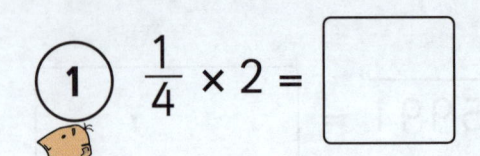

1) $\frac{1}{4} \times 2 =$

2) $4 \times 1\frac{1}{7} =$

3) $3 \times 1\frac{1}{3} =$

4) $3\frac{2}{5} \times 2 =$

5) $3 \times \frac{2}{5} =$

6) $1\frac{1}{4} \times 6 =$

7) $5 \times 2\frac{2}{3} =$

8) $3\frac{2}{9} \times 5 =$

9) $3 \times 1\frac{5}{6} =$

10) $2\frac{4}{7} \times 8 =$

11) $12 \times \frac{4}{5} =$

12) $2\frac{3}{8} \times 7 =$

Today I scored ☐ out of 12.

Answers

Week 1 — Day 1
1. $\frac{1}{2}$
2. $\frac{1}{4}$
3. $\frac{4}{10}$
4. $\frac{3}{4}$
5. $\frac{3}{10}$
6. $\frac{1}{5}$
7. $\frac{45}{100}$
8. $\frac{2}{8}$
9. $\frac{65}{100}$
10. $\frac{90}{100}$

Week 1 — Day 2
1. 1
2. −3
3. 5
4. −2
5. −7
6. −8
7. 0
8. 4
9. −9
10. 2

Week 1 — Day 3
1. 5
2. 6
3. 5
4. 0
5. 10
6. 7

Week 1 — Day 4
1. 40 403, 50 403, 60 403, **70 403**, **80 403**, **90 403**
2. 3929, 3949, 3969, **3989**, **4009**, **4029**
3. 17 229, 16 229, 15 229, **14 229**, **13 229**, **12 229**
4. 7536, 7836, 8136, **8436**, **8736**, **9036**
5. 442, 1542, 2642, **3742**, **4842**, **5942**
6. 88 922, 87 921, 86 920, **85 919**, **84 918**, **83 917**
7. 66 823, 75 823, 84 823, **93 823**, **102 823**, **111 823**
8. 7216, 7616, 8016, **8416**, **8816**, **9216**

Week 1 — Day 5
1. Cam
2. Fia
3. Hugh
4. Ike
5. Kat
6. Mo
7. Ola
8. Quin
9. Sid
10. Una

Week 2 — Day 1
1. 30 000
2. 50 000
3. 60 000
4. 700 000
5. 800 000
6. 300 000
7. 300 000
8. 390 000
9. 440 000
10. 250 000
11. 1 000 000
12. 900 000

Week 2 — Day 2
1. $\frac{1}{3}, \frac{2}{6}, \frac{4}{12}$
2. $\frac{4}{24}, \frac{3}{18}, \frac{1}{6}$
3. $\frac{1}{5}, \frac{2}{10}$
4. $\frac{3}{10}, \frac{9}{30}$
5. $\frac{2}{5}, \frac{4}{10}$
6. $\frac{4}{9}, \frac{12}{27}$
7. $\frac{2}{8}, \frac{6}{24}$
8. $\frac{4}{14}, \frac{12}{42}, \frac{2}{7}$

Week 2 — Day 3
1. 1208
2. 1343
3. 1012
4. 1663
5. 952
6. 1049
7. 1503
8. 925

Week 2 — Day 4
1. 830, 8.3
2. × 10, 47 000
3. 160, 0.16
4. × 1000, ÷ 100
5. 0.9, ÷ 10
6. 16.5, 1650
7. 3.24, 32.4
8. ÷100, 25

Week 2 — Day 5
1. £6.20
2. £7.85
3. £3.85
4. £5.15
5. £6.49
6. £12.45

Week 3 — Day 1
1. 50
2. 4
3. 15
4. 23
5. 56
6. 90
7. 77
8. 88
9. 91
10. 99
11. 49
12. 79

Week 3 — Day 2
1. 100 cm
2. 1 l
3. 0.1 kg
4. 5 m
5. 3000 ml
6. 0.02 kg
7. 5 cm
8. 0.456 l
9. 8400 g
10. 5510 ml
11. 2.998 kg
12. 0.6 m

Week 3 — Day 3
1. 8486
2. 4183
3. 97 777
4. 52 867
5. 10 909
6. 72 199
7. 78 889
8. 73 220
9. 2346
10. 93 221

Week 3 — Day 4
1. 10
2. 32
3. 26
4. 30
5. 15
6. 72
7. 11
8. 98
9. 24
10. 96

Week 3 — Day 5
1. −1
2. −1
3. 8
4. 5
5. 7
6. 7
7. −4
8. −6
9. −2
10. −9
11. 11
12. 6

Week 4 — Day 1
1. 8892 − 5842 = 3150 or
   8892 − 3150 = 5842
2. 4260 + 3452 = 7712 or
   3452 + 4260 = 7712
3. 9449 − 2998 = 6451 or
   9449 − 6451 = 2998
4. 4584 + 4443 = 9027 or
   4443 + 4584 = 9027
5. 5010 ÷ 501 = 10 or
   5010 ÷ 10 = 501
6. 106 × 6 = 636 or
   6 × 106 = 636
7. 968 ÷ 4 = 242 or
   968 ÷ 242 = 4
8. 124 × 8 = 992 or
   8 × 124 = 992

Week 4 — Day 2
1. 90°
2. 30°
3. 150°
4. 45°
5. 80°
6. 130°
7. 60°
8. 60°
9. 110°
10. 170°

Week 4 — Day 3
1. 9
2. 10
3. 16
4. 27
5. 26
6. 13
7. 14
8. 21
9. 94
10. 27

Week 4 — Day 4
1. 10 cm
2. 500 g
3. 4 l
4. 12 pints
5. 10 inches
6. 1 ounce
7. 25 l
8. 15 inches
9. 30 ounces
10. 55 cm

Week 4 — Day 5
1. 1550
2. 4015
3. 2736
4. 1763
5. 351
6. 832

Week 5 — Day 1
1. 3700
2. 25
3. 8
4. 12
5. 7.8
6. 6540
7. 1.5
8. 40
9. 4.83
10. 3983
11. 44.97
12. 79 380

Week 5 — Day 2
1. $\frac{2}{3}$
2. $\frac{5}{6}$
3. $\frac{10}{7}$ or $1\frac{3}{7}$
4. $\frac{8}{7}$ or $1\frac{1}{7}$
5. $\frac{19}{12}$ or $1\frac{7}{12}$
6. $\frac{10}{3}$ or $3\frac{1}{3}$
7. $\frac{3}{4}$
8. $\frac{23}{7}$ or $3\frac{2}{7}$
9. $\frac{1}{9}$
10. $\frac{13}{8}$ or $1\frac{5}{8}$
11. $\frac{23}{6}$ or $3\frac{5}{6}$
12. $\frac{29}{5}$ or $5\frac{4}{5}$

Week 5 — Day 3
1. Three thousand eight hundred and twenty nine
2. Fifteen thousand one hundred and seven
3. Seventy six thousand five hundred and ninety one
4. Forty four thousand and sixty six
5. One hundred and twelve thousand
6. Eight hundred and eight thousand, nine hundred and eighty seven
7. One hundred thousand, one hundred
8. Nine hundred and ninety nine thousand, nine hundred and ninety nine
9. One hundred and twenty three thousand, four hundred and fifty six
10. Four hundred and forty thousand and thirty three

Week 5 — Day 4
1. 07:35
2. 08:41
3. 09:36
4. 11:56
5. 12:16

Week 5 — Day 5
1. 270
2. 30
3. $2\frac{1}{2}$
4. 135
5. $6\frac{1}{4}$
6. 105
7. $7\frac{3}{4}$
8. 200

Week 6 — Day 1
1. 19:20
2. 02:30
3. 5:35 pm
4. 8:01 pm
5. 23:59
6. 11:00
7. 18:30
8. 10:47 pm
9. 7:27 pm
10. 1:13 pm
11. 00:05
12. 12:39

Week 6 — Day 2
1. $\frac{37}{100}, \frac{38}{100}, \frac{39}{100}$
2. 0.29, 0.31, 0.33
3. $\frac{40}{100}, \frac{45}{100}, \frac{50}{100}$
4. 0.74, 0.72, 0.7
5. 1, 1.25, 1.5
6. $\frac{32}{100}, \frac{28}{100}, \frac{24}{100}$

Week 6 — Day 3
1. 21.4 km
2. 21 km
3. 24.2 km
4. 12 km
5. 0.5 km
6. 4 km
7. 1 km
8. 4.5 km
9. 3.8 km
10. 4.2 km

Week 6 — Day 4
1. 900 ml
2. 600 g
3. 100 ml
4. 2 kg
5. 200 ml
6. 100 g
7. 240 g
8. 1.25 l

Week 6 — Day 5
1. 3
2. 4
3. 8
4. 9
5. 7
6. 14
7. 2
8. 7

Week 7 — Day 1

1. $\frac{9}{2}$
2. $\frac{17}{3}$
3. $\frac{31}{5}$
4. $\frac{83}{10}$
5. $\frac{30}{7}$
6. $\frac{61}{6}$
7. $\frac{19}{11}$
8. $\frac{52}{9}$
9. $\frac{65}{12}$
10. $\frac{47}{6}$
11. $\frac{51}{8}$
12. $\frac{77}{9}$

Week 7 — Day 2

1. 80
2. 2500
3. 70
4. 200
5. 8
6. 2600
7. 200
8. 70
9. 360
10. 270
11. 3200
12. 60

Week 7 — Day 3

1. $\frac{10}{23}$
2. $\frac{8}{27}$
3. $\frac{9}{29}$
4. $\frac{8}{52}$ or $\frac{2}{13}$
5. $\frac{22}{58}$ or $\frac{11}{29}$
6. $\frac{12}{54}$ or $\frac{2}{9}$

Week 7 — Day 4

1. $\frac{5}{6}$
2. $\frac{3}{10}$
3. $\frac{9}{12}$ or $\frac{3}{4}$
4. $1\frac{1}{8}$
5. $\frac{5}{9}$
6. $1\frac{26}{100}$ or $1\frac{13}{50}$
7. $\frac{18}{50}$ or $\frac{9}{25}$
8. $1\frac{3}{16}$
9. $\frac{23}{36}$
10. $1\frac{11}{35}$
11. $\frac{5}{18}$
12. $\frac{62}{100}$ or $\frac{31}{50}$

Week 7 — Day 5

1. 70 cm
2. 107 cm
3. 50 cm
4. 46 cm
5. 64 cm
6. 138 cm

Week 8 — Day 1

1. 69 589
2. 44 450
3. 41 110
4. 94 230
5. 56 394
6. 9999
7. 41 214
8. 36 878
9. 74 311
10. 42 889
11. 65 423
12. 1468

Week 8 — Day 2

1. 43°
2. 100°
3. 16°
4. 48°
5. 27°
6. 51°
7. 28°
8. 99°

Week 8 — Day 3

1. 18
2. 45
3. 48
4. 44
5. 84
6. 108
7. 72
8. 132

Week 8 — Day 4

1. 320
2. 400
3. 780
4. 1100
5. 860
6. 800
7. 250
8. 140

Week 8 — Day 5

1. 17:59
2. 19:20
3. 17:03
4. 17:50
5. 18:52

Week 9 — Day 1

1. 15 145
2. 5226
3. 48 280
4. 1 081 123
5. 205 765
6. 26 428
7. 1412
8. 100 139
9. 27 401
10. 65 261
11. 35 189
12. 104 323

Week 9 — Day 2

1. Square/(regular) quadrilateral 
2. Equilateral (regular) triangle 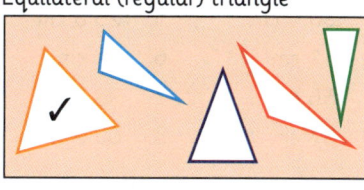
3. (Regular) hexagon 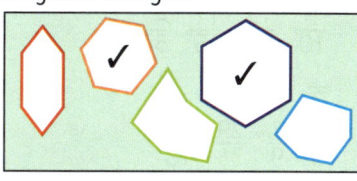
4. (Regular) octagon 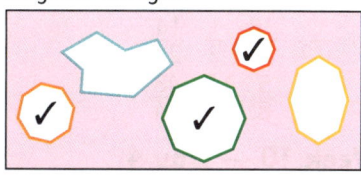
5. (Regular) heptagon 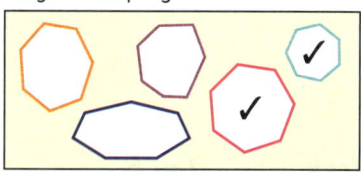
6. (Regular) decagon

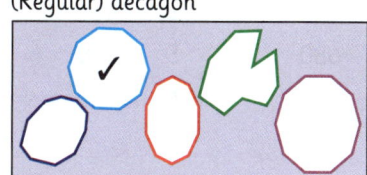

Week 9 — Day 3

1. 2 m
2. 10 cm
3. 9 cm
4. 15 mm
5. 7 m
6. 5 m

Week 9 — Day 4

1. 3
2. 2, 5
3. 7
4. 3, 6
5. 2, 4, 8
6. 5
7. 1, 3, 9
8. 1, 2, 8, 16

Week 9 — Day 5

1. 30°
2. 66°
3. 48°
4. 36°
5. 18°
6. 45°
7. 59°
8. 58°

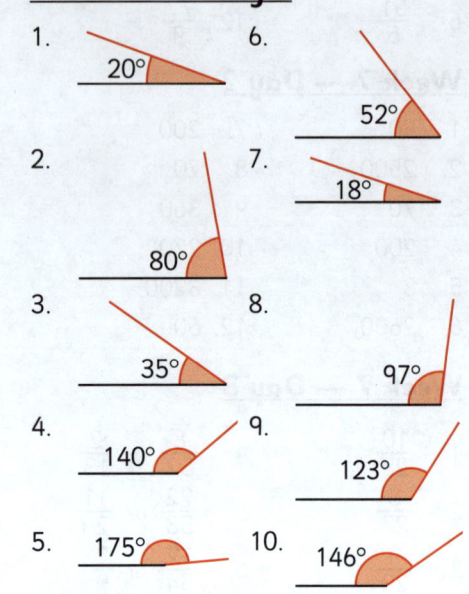

Week 10 — Day 1
1. 9 p
2. 52 p
3. 30 p
4. 90 p
5. 23 p
6. 13 p
7. 26 p
8. 55 p

Week 10 — Day 2
1. 30.4 cm
2. 51 cm
3. 56.4 cm
4. 37 cm
5. 25.8 cm
6. 74 cm
7. 38 cm
8. 63.2 cm

Week 10 — Day 3
1. $\frac{2}{10}$ $\frac{12}{30}$ $\frac{11}{15}$ $\frac{4}{5}$
2. $\frac{1}{2}$ $\frac{11}{20}$ $\frac{23}{40}$ $\frac{6}{10}$
3. $\frac{2}{3}$ $\frac{7}{9}$ $\frac{29}{36}$ $\frac{16}{18}$
4. $\frac{11}{30}$ $\frac{2}{5}$ $\frac{25}{60}$ $\frac{12}{15}$
5. $\frac{2}{12}$ $\frac{18}{72}$ $\frac{1}{3}$ $\frac{14}{24}$
6. $\frac{19}{32}$ $\frac{5}{8}$ $\frac{11}{16}$ $\frac{48}{64}$

Week 10 — Day 4
1. 66 cm^2
2. 130 cm^2
3. 90 cm^2
4. 112 cm^2
5. 154 cm^2
6. 171 cm^2
7. 300 cm^2
8. 442 cm^2

Week 10 — Day 5
1. 156
2. 680
3. 612
4. 1519
5. 1408
6. 792

Week 11 — Day 1
1. Triangular prism
2. Cuboid
3. Cylinder
4. Square-based pyramid
5. Triangle-based pyramid
6. Cone

Week 11 — Day 2
1. C, 2°C
2. E, 5°C
3. G, 4°C
4. I, 5°C

Week 11 — Day 3
1. 17 900
2. 18 820
3. 29 743
4. 1 590 000
5. 3 290 000
6. 5 153 000
7. 875 000
8. 71 500
9. 685 500
10. 451 700
11. 1 319 000
12. 2 318 000

Week 11 — Day 4
1. 12 cm^3
2. 24 cm^3
3. 20 cm^3
4. 36 cm^3
5. 30 cm^3
6. 22 cm^3
7. 16 cm^3
8. 36 cm^3

Week 11 — Day 5
1. £18.20
2. £20.30
3. £33.90
4. £55.44
5. £25.98
6. £48.56

Week 12 — Day 1
1. 7.7
2. 0.8
3. 6.1
4. 4.5
5. 8.7
6. 5.0
7. 0.4
8. 1.2
9. 3.6
10. 10.0
11. 6.9
12. 0.5

Week 12 — Day 2
1. 20°
2. 80°
3. 35°
4. 140°
5. 175°
6. 52°
7. 18°
8. 97°
9. 123°
10. 146°

Week 12 — Day 3
1. 1 l
2. 1651 kg
3. 1 kg
4. 0 g
5. 84 l
6. 64 m
7. 332 ml
8. 383 cm

Week 12 — Day 4
1. 9960
2. 1456 r 3
3. 33 705
4. 284 r 4
5. 18 781
6. 748 r 7
7. 49 038
8. 687 r 1
9. 54 109
10. 1387 r 4

Week 12 — Day 5
1. $\frac{1}{2}$
2. $4\frac{4}{7}$
3. 4
4. $6\frac{4}{5}$
5. $1\frac{1}{5}$
6. $7\frac{1}{2}$
7. $13\frac{1}{3}$
8. $16\frac{1}{9}$
9. $5\frac{1}{2}$
10. $20\frac{4}{7}$
11. $9\frac{3}{5}$
12. $16\frac{5}{8}$

Answers